ALSO BY MARGE PIERCY

Poetry

Early Grrrl

What Are Big Girls Made Of?

Mars and Her Children

Available Light

My Mother's Body

Stone, Paper, Knife

Circles on the Water

The Moon Is Always Female

The Twelve-Spoked Wheel Flashing

Living in the Open

To Be of Use

4-Telling *(with Robert Hershon, Emmett Jarrett, Dick Lourie)*

Hard Loving

Breaking Camp

Novels

Storm Tide *(with Ira Wood)*

City of Darkness, City of Light

The Longings of Women

He, She and It

Summer People

Gone to Soldiers

Fly Away Home

Braided Lives

Vida

The High Cost of Living

Woman on the Edge of Time

Small Changes

Dance the Eagle to Sleep

Going Down Fast

Other

The Last White Class: A Play *(with Ira Wood)*

Parti-Colored Blocks for a Quilt: Essays

Early Ripening: American Women's Poetry Now: An Anthology

The Earth Shines Secretly: A Book of Days *(with paintings by Nell Blaine)*

The Art of
Blessing the Day

The Art of Blessing the Day

POEMS WITH A JEWISH THEME

Marge Piercy

ALFRED A. KNOPF   New York   1999

THIS IS A BORZOI BOOK
PUBLISHED BY ALFRED A. KNOPF, INC.

Copyright © 1999 by Middlemarsh, Inc.

www.randomhouse.com

Acknowledgments of previous publication
of the poems may be found on page 177.

Library of Congress Cataloging-in-Publication Data
Piercy, Marge.
The art of blessing the day : poems with a Jewish theme /
by Marge Piercy. — 1st ed.
p.   cm.
ISBN 0-375-40477-5 (alk. paper)
1. Jewish religious poetry, American. 2. Jewish
families—Poetry. 3. Jews—Poetry. I. Title.
PS3566.I4A89   1999
811'.54—dc21   98-14207
          CIP

Manufactured in the United States of America
First Edition

*For all who may find here poems that speak to their identity,
their history, their desire for ritual—ritual that may work for them—
these poems are yours as well as mine*

Contents

HA-SHANAH *(The Year)*

The Art of
Blessing the Day

The art of blessing the day

This is the blessing for rain after drought:
Come down, wash the air so it shimmers,
a perfumed shawl of lavender chiffon.
Let the parched leaves suckle and swell.
Enter my skin, wash me for the little
chrysalis of sleep rocked in your plashing.
In the morning the world is peeled to shining.

This is the blessing for sun after long rain:
Now everything shakes itself free and rises.
The trees are bright as pushcart ices.
Every last lily opens its satin thighs.
The bees dance and roll in pollen
and the cardinal at the top of the pine
sings at full throttle, fountaining.

This is the blessing for a ripe peach:
This is luck made round. Frost can nip
the blossom, kill the bee. It can drop,
a hard green useless nut. Brown fungus,
the burrowing worm that coils in rot can
blemish it and wind crush it on the ground.
Yet this peach fills my mouth with juicy sun.

This is the blessing for the first garden tomato:
Those green boxes of tasteless acid the store

sells in January, those red things with the savor
of wet chalk, they mock your fragrant name.
How fat and sweet you are weighing down my palm,
warm as the flank of a cow in the sun.
You are the savor of summer in a thin red skin.

This is the blessing for a political victory:
Although I shall not forget that things
work in increments and epicycles and sometime
leaps that half the time fall back down,
let's not relinquish dancing while the music
fits into our hips and bounces our heels.
We must never forget, pleasure is real as pain.

The blessing for the return of a favorite cat,
the blessing for love returned, for friends'
return, for money received unexpected,
the blessing for the rising of the bread,
the sun, the oppressed. I am not sentimental
about old men mumbling the Hebrew by rote
with no more feeling than one says gesundheit.

But the discipline of blessings is to taste
each moment, the bitter, the sour, the sweet
and the salty, and be glad for what does not
hurt. The art is in compressing attention
to each little and big blossom of the tree

of life, to let the tongue sing each fruit,
its savor, its aroma and its use.

Attention is love, what we must give
children, mothers, fathers, pets,
our friends, the news, the woes of others.
What we want to change we curse and then
pick up a tool. Bless whatever you can
with eyes and hands and tongue. If you
can't bless it, get ready to make it new.

Mishpocheh

(FAMILY)

Snowflakes, my mother called them

Snowflakes, my mother called them.
My grandmother made papercuts
until she was too blind to see
the intricate birds, trees, Mogen
Davids, moons, flowers
that appeared like magic
when the folded paper
was opened.

My mother made simpler ones,
abstract. She never saved them.
Not hers, not mine.
It was a winter game.
Usually we had only newsprint
to play with. Sometimes
we used old wrapping paper,
white sheets from the bakery.

Often Grandma tacked hers
to the walls or on the window
that looked on the street,
the east window where the sun
rose hidden behind tenements
where she faced to pray.
I remember one with deer,
delicate hooves, fine antlers

for Pesach. Her animals were
always in pairs, the rabbits,

the cats, always cats in pairs,
little mice, but never horses,
for horses meant pogrom,
the twice widowed woman's
sense of how things should be,
even trees by twos for company.

I had forgotten. I had lost it all
until a woman sent me a papercut
to thank me for a poem, and then
in my hand I felt a piece of past
materialize, a snowflake long melted,
evaporated, cohering and once
again tower-necked fragile deer
stood, made of skill and absence.

Putting the good things away

In the drawer were folded fine
batiste slips embroidered with scrolls
and posies, edged with handmade
lace too good for her to wear.

Daily she put on shmattehs
fit only to wash the car
or the windows, rags
that had never been pretty

even when new: somewhere
such dresses are sold only
to women without money to waste
on themselves, on pleasure,

to women who hate their bodies,
to women whose lives close on them.
Such dresses come bleached by tears,
packed in salt like herring.

Yet she put the good things away
for the good day that must surely
come, when promises would open
like tulips their satin cups

for her to drink the sweet
sacramental wine of fulfillment.

The story shone in her as through
tinted glass, how the mother

gave up and did without
and was in the end crowned
with what? scallions? crowned
queen of the dead place

in the heart where old dreams
whistle on bone flutes,
where run-over pets are forgotten,
where lost stockings go?

In the coffin she was beautiful
not because of the undertaker's
garish cosmetics but because
that face at eighty was still

her face at eighteen peering
over the drab long dress
of poverty, clutching a book.
Where did you read your dreams, Mother?

Because her expression softened
from the pucker of disappointment,
the grimace of swallowed rage,
she looked a white-haired girl.

The anger turned inward, the anger

turned inward, where
could it go except to make pain?
It flowed into me with her milk.

Her anger annealed me.
I was dipped into the cauldron
of boiling rage and rose
a warrior and a witch

but still vulnerable
there where she held me.
She could always wound me
for she knew the secret places.

She could always touch me
for she knew the pressure
points of pleasure and pain.
Our minds were woven together.

I gave her presents and she hid
them away, wrapped in plastic.
Too good, she said, too good.
I'm saving them. So after her death

I sort them, the ugly things
that were sufficient for every
day and the pretty things for which
no day of hers was ever good enough.

Eat fruit

Keep your legs crossed, Mother said. Drinking
leads to babies. Don't hang around street corners.
I rushed to gulp moonshine on corners, hip outthrust.
So why in the butter of my brain does one marble tablet
shine bearing my mother's commandment, eat fruit?

Here I stand, the only poet from whom
you can confidently obtain after a reading
enough mushy tan bananas to bake bread
should you happen to feel the urge at ten
some night in East Lansing or Boise.

You understand how needful it is, you say,
that I should carry the products of Cape
Cod such as oranges and kiwis with me
because surely they sell none in Seattle.
Suppose South America should be blockaded?

Others litter ash, beer cans. I leak pits.
As we descend into Halifax while my seat partner
is snorting the last of his coke, I am the one
choking as I gobble three apples in five minutes,
agricultural contraband seized at borders.

Customs agents throw open my suitcase and draw
out with gingerly leer from under my negligee

a melon. Drug smugglers feed their self-importance,
but me they hate along with the guy trying to smuggle
in a salami from the old country his uncle gave him.

I am the slob who makes gory stains on railroad seats
with fermenting strawberries. You can recognize me
by the happy cloud of winged creatures following my
   head.
I have raised more fruitflies than genetics labs.
I have endowed ant orphanages and retirement
   communities.

However, I tell you smugly, I am regular in Nome,
in Paducah, in both Portlands and all Springfields.
While you are eating McMuffins I am savoring a bruised
but extremely sophisticated pear that has seen five
airports and four cities and grown old in wisdom.

Learning to read

My mother would not teach me to read.
Experts in newspapers and pop books
said school must receive us virgin.
Secrets were locked in those

black scribbles on white, magic
to open the sky and the earth.
In a book I tried to guess from
pictures, a mountain had in its side

a door through which children ran in
after a guy playing a flute
dressed all in green, and I too
wanted to march into a mountain.

When I sat at Grandmother's seder,
the book went around and everybody
read. I did not make a distinction
between languages. Half the words

in English were strange to me.
I knew when I had learned to read
all would be clear, I would know
everything that adults knew, and more.

Every handle would turn for me.
At school I grabbed words like toys
I had been denied. Finally I
could read, me. I read every sign

from the car. On journeys I read
maps. I read every cereal box
and can, spelling out the hard words.
All printing was sacred.

At the seder I sat down at the table,
self-important, adult on my cushion.
I was no longer the youngest child
but the smartest. When the Haggadah

was to be passed across me,
I grabbed it, roaring confidence.
But the squiggles, the scratches
were back. Not a letter

waved to me. I was blinded again.
That night I learned about tongues.
Grandma explained she herself spoke
Yiddish, Russian, Polish, Lithuanian

and bad English, little Hebrew.
That's okay, I said. I will

learn all languages. But I was
fifty before I read Hebrew.

I no longer expect to master
every alphabet before death
snatches away everything I know.
But they are always beckoning to me

those languages still squiggles
and noises, like lovers I never
had time to enjoy, places
I have never (yet) arrived.

My mother's body

1.

The dark socket of the year
the pit, the cave where the sun lies down
and threatens never to rise,
when despair descends softly as the snow
covering all paths and choking roads:

then hawkfaced pain seized you
threw you so you fell with a sharp
cry, a knife tearing a bolt of silk.
My father heard the crash but paid
no mind, napping after lunch

yet fifteen hundred miles north
I heard and dropped a dish.
Your pain sunk talons in my skull
and crouched there cawing, heavy
as a great vessel filled with water,

oil or blood, till suddenly next day
the weight lifted and I knew your mind
had guttered out like the Chanukah
candles that burn so fast, weeping
veils of wax down the chanukiya.

Those candles were laid out,
friends invited, ingredients bought
for latkes and apple pancakes,

that holiday for liberation
and the winter solstice

when tops turn like little planets.
Shall you have all or nothing
take half or pass by untouched?
Nothing you got, *Nun* said the dreydl
as the room stopped spinning.

The angel folded you up like laundry
your body thin as an empty dress.
Your clothes were curtains
hanging on the window of what had
been your flesh and now was glass.

Outside in Florida shopping plazas
loudspeakers blared Christmas carols
and palm trees were decked with blinking
lights. Except by the tourist
hotels, the beaches were empty.

Pelicans with pregnant pouches
flapped overhead like dinosaurs.
In my mind I felt you die.
First the pain lifted and then
you flickered and went out.

2.

I walk through the rooms of memory.
Sometimes everything is shrouded in dropcloths,
every chair ghostly and muted.

Other times memory lights up from within
bustling scenes acted just the other side
of a scrim through which surely I could reach

my fingers tearing at the flimsy curtain
of time which is and isn't and will be
the stuff of which we're made and unmade.

In sleep the other night I met you, seventeen
your first nasty marriage just annulled,
thin from your abortion, clutching a book

against your cheek and trying to look
older, trying to look middle class,
trying for a job at Wanamaker's

dressing for parties in cast off
stage costumes of your sisters. Your eyes
were hazy with dreams. You did not

notice me waving as you wandered
past and I saw your slip was showing.
You stood still while I fixed your clothes,

as if I were your mother. Remember me
combing your springy black hair, ringlets
that seemed metallic, glittering;

remember me dressing you, my seventy year
old mother who was my last dollbaby,
giving you too late what your youth had wanted.

3.

What is this mask of skin we wear,
what is this dress of flesh,
this coat of few colors and little hair?

This voluptuous seething heap of desires
and fears squeaking, mice turned up
in a steaming haystack with their babies?

This coat has been handed down, an heirloom
this coat of black hair and ample flesh,
this coat of pale slightly ruddy skin.

This set of hips and thighs, these buttocks
they provided cushioning for my grandmother
Hannah, for my mother Bert and for me

and we all sat on them in turn, those major
muscles on which we walk and walk and walk
over the earth in search of peace and plenty.

My mother is my mirror and I am hers.
What do we see? Our face grown young again,
our breasts grown firm, legs lean and elegant.

Our arms quivering with fat, eyes
set in the bark of wrinkles, hands puffy,
our belly seamed with childbearing,

Give me your dress that I might try it on.
Oh it will not fit you mother, you are too fat.
I will not fit you mother.

I will not be the bride you can dress,
the obedient dutiful daughter you would chew,
a dog's leather bone to sharpen your teeth.

You strike me sometimes just to hear the sound.
Loneliness turns your fingers into hooks
barbed and drawing blood with their caress.

My twin, my sister, my lost love,
I carry you in me like an embryo
as once you carried me.

4.

What is it we turn from, what is it we fear?
Did I truly think you could put me back inside?
Did I think I would fall into you as into a molten

furnace and be recast, that I would become you?

What did you fear in me, the child who wore
your hair, the woman who let that black hair
grow long as a banner of darkness, when you
a proper flapper wore yours cropped.

You pushed and you pulled on my rubbery
flesh, you kneaded me like a ball of dough.
Rise, rise, and then you pounded me flat.
Secretly the bones formed in the bread.

I became willful, private as a cat.
You never knew what alleys I had wandered.
You called me bad and I posed like a gutter
queen in a dress sewn of knives.

All I feared was being stuck in a box
with a lid. A good woman appeared to me
indistinguishable from a dead one
except that she worked all the time.

Your payday never came. Your dreams ran
with bright colors like Mexican cottons
that bled onto the drab sheets of the day
and would not bleach with scrubbing.

My dear, what you said was one thing
but what you sang was another, sweetly

subversive and dark as blackberries
and I became the daughter of your dream.

This body is your body, ashes now
and roses, but alive in my eyes, my breasts,
my throat, my thighs. You run in me
a tang of salt in the creek waters of my blood,

you sing in my mind like wine. What you
did not dare in your life you dare in mine.

On shabbat she dances
in the candle flames

How we danced then, you can't imagine
my grandmother said. We danced
till we were dizzy, we danced
till the room spun like a dreydl,
we danced ourselves drunk and giddy,
we danced till we fell panting.

We were poor, my grandmother said,
a few potatoes, some half rotten
beans, greens from the hedgerow.
But then on shabbat we ate a chicken.
The candles shone on the golden skin.
We drank sweet wine and flew up to the ceiling.

How I loved him, you can't imagine
my grandmother said. He was from St.
Petersberg, my father could scarcely
believe he was a Jew, he dressed so fine.
His eyes burned when he looked at me.
He quoted Pushkin instead of Mishnah.

Nine languages and still the Czar
wanted him in the Army, where Jews
went off but never returned.
My father married us from his deathbed.

We escaped under a load of straw.
You can't imagine, we were frightened mice.

Eleven children I bore, my grandmother said,
nine who grew up, four who died
before me. Now I sing in your ear.
When you pray I stand beside you.
Elijah's cup at the seder table is for
me, who cooked and never sat down:

now I sit enthroned on your computer.
Now I am the queen of dustmop tales,
I preside over your memory lighting
candles that summon the dead.
I touch your lids while you sleep
and when you wake, you imagine me.

The wicked stepmother

1. Change of personnel

The good and loving mother dies;
the stepmother usurps her bed,
begins punishing unjustly,
steals away the honey and chocolate;
gives vinegar and ashes.

It does not happen in infancy.
No, you are cuddled to breasts
whose softness will always
haunt you, whose sweetness
is a mirage in every bed.

It begins in late childhood.
It begins with bitter
policing, acid of resentment:
how dare you turn on me, my
child, and grow apple breasts?

It begins with the grating
of mistrust rubbing the mind raw.
It begins with arcane rules.
Don't sit with your legs spread.
Don't you dare walk that way.

It begins with suspicions
multiplying like mice, nibbling

in the night, leaving little
turds in everything nice, the kit-
chen once bathed in milky light.

Who is this woman who stands
at the foot of the bed denouncing?
Who is this woman who ransacks
diaries, drawers, listens
on the extension, cross-examines?

This is the wicked stepmother
the long toothed wolf who gobbled
Mommy. This is the basic
female betrayal, that the first
lover becomes the queen of No.

2. Change of personal pronoun

For years, holidays were in-
quisition time. Me the foul
roasting on the spit. Your
anger the roaring fire.

For years, every choice I
made was suspect. Was I
really a writer, was I
really married, was I

actually going to Greece,
Mexico, Czechoslovakia, France.
You will die in a gutter,
you said, with your throat slit.

Was there a synonym for slut
you missed? Yiddish, English
your tongue was a thesaurus
of sexual insult, my sins

too gross for any slipper
no matter how mammoth.
Then when you turned eighty
suddenly she was back

the mother of all memory,
the dark warm fragrant rose
surrounding me. Oh, Mother,
you returned to love me again
just before the end of time.

The rabbi's granddaughter
and the Christmas tree

Mother, the rabbi's granddaughter, wanted Christmas.
It was not Jesus she hankered for, not carols
or masses or mangers. She wanted the bright
lights of trees glittering and she wanted presents.

She loved light. All through the brownout
of the war, she waited. When peace came,
Father drove the old Hudson past trimmed
big brick houses, colonials, ranches

in neat rows on streets so unlike our own
they might have been toy houses in store
windows downtown. She wanted to see colored
bulbs blinking, she wanted to glide,

a connoisseur of the gaudy, awarding prizes.
We dragged out a box of paper folded, saved
from last year and the year before. Old
friends. Mourned when too tattered.

She would buy herself a sweater and wrap
it: a gift from my father, who did not
bother. The actual presents were always
cheesy. No money to waste. I got

socks, mittens. We ironed the ribbons
to use again. A charade of giving,
what you asked for never came.
What you got was the box, packed

carefully away for the next year
when it would appear again like a bad
comedian to tell the same dismal joke.
It's the spirit, she said, that counts.

After I left home, I never put up a tree
until she was dying. Then she gave me
a box of flimsy glass ornaments, some
half a century old. Use them, she said,

be observant but set up a tree.
I want to see the lights. As I go into
darkness, I don't want a stone. Only
red, gold and blue shining for me.

What she craved

My mother sugared grapefruit;
my father salted it.
My mother sugared cantaloupe;
my father salted it.

My mother put sugar and lemon
on leaf lettuce from her garden;
two heaping teaspoonfuls into
her milky coffee, with cake.

Her teeth rotted out and were
yanked from her bleeding jaws
by a cheap sadist downtown.
Still she craved sweetness.

In a life with too much that
was bitter, tear soaked salty,
sour as unspoken grief,
sugar was her comfort

a little sweetness in the mouth
lingering like an infrequent kiss;
sugar was the friend kept her clock
ticking through running down days.

Unbuttoning

The buttons lie jumbled in a tin
that once held good lapsang souchong
tea from China, smoky as the smell
from a wood stove in the country,
leaves opening to flavor and fate.

As I turn buttons over, they sound
like strange money being counted
toward a purchase as I point
dumbly in a foreign bazaar,
coins pittering from my hand.

Buttons are told with the fingers
like worry beads as I search
the trove for something small
and red to fill the missing
slot on a blouse placket.

I carried them from my mother's
sewing table, a wise legacy
not only practical but better
able than fading snapshots
to conjure buried seasons.

Button stamped with an anchor
means my late grade-school pea coat.
Button in the form of a white
daisy from a sky blue dress
she wore, splashed with that flower,

rouses her face like a rosy dahlia
bent over me petaled with curls.
O sunflower hungry for joy
who turned her face through the years
bleak, withered, still yearning.

The tea was a present I brought
her from New York where she
had never gone and never would.
This mauve nub's from a dress
once drenched in her blood.

This, from a coral dress she wore
the day she taught me that word,
summer '41, in Florida:
"Watch the clipper ships take off
for Europe. Soon war will come to us.

"They will not rise so peacefully
for years. Over there they're
killing us and nobody cares.
Remember always. Coral is built
of bodies of the dead piled up."

Buttons are useful little monuments.
They fasten and keep decently
shut and warm. They also open.
Rattling in my hand, they're shells
left by vanished flesh.

Out of the rubbish

Among my mother's things I found
a bottle-cap flower: the top
from a ginger ale
into which had been glued
crystalline beads from a necklace
surrounding a blue bauble.

It is not unattractive,
this star-shaped posy
in the wreath of fluted
aluminum, but it is not
as a thing of beauty
that I carried it off.

A receding vista opens
of workingclass making do:
the dress that becomes
a blouse that becomes
a dolldress, potholders,
rags to wash windows.

Petunias in the tire.
Remnants of old rugs
laid down over the holes
in rugs that had once

been new when the rem-
nants were first old.

A three-inch birchbark
canoe labeled Muskegon,
little wooden shoes
souvenirs of Holland, Mich.,
an ashtray from the Blue Hole
reputed bottomless.

Look out the window
at the sulphur sky.
The street is grey as
newspapers. Rats
waddle up the alley.
The air is brown.

If we make curtains
of the rose-bedecked table
cloth, the stain won't show
and it will be cheerful,
cheerful. Paint the wall lime.
Paint it turquoise, primrose.

How I used to dream
in Detroit of deep cobalt,
of ochre reds, of cadmium
yellow. I dreamed of sea

and burning sun, of red
islands and blue volcanos.

After she washed the floors
she used to put down newspapers
to keep them clean. When
the newspapers had become
dirty, the floor beneath
was no longer clean.

In the window, ceramic
bunnies sprouted cactus.
A burro offered fuchsia.
In the hat, a wandering Jew.
That was your grandfather.
He spoke nine languages.

Don't you ever want to
travel? *I did when I*
was younger. Now, what
would be the point?
Who would want to meet me?
I'd be ashamed.

One night alone she sat
at her kitchen table
glueing baubles in a cap.
When she had finished,
pleased, she hid it away
where no one could see.

Your father's fourth heart attack

The phone cord is the umbilicus
that binds him dying, shriveled,
to you his first son.
You try to draw him to you.
You give him advice. I hear

your voice tender, careful,
admonishing, arguing.
You ask him ten polite ways
why he is killing himself
by the teaspoonful, by the drop,

by the puff. Why he eats
ashes instead of apples,
why he sucks on death's
icy dry tit, why he turns
his face into darkness.

You cajole him, a step, a step
like a father coaxing a toddler,
but he falls through your fingers
into a maze of knives giving him
his face back screaming.

Twelve hours a day he worked,
four hours commuting, up nights
in a chair by TV late show light
wolfing burnt steak and salami on rye,
counting other men's paychecks.

He lived among men with boats,
sleek men, slick men, always richer.
He bought a boat from a moneyed neighbor,
fiberglass hulled, had it repaired,
started it, roared out and sank.

No place he lived was ever right,
but he was always talking up the next
move. He quarreled with brothers,
mother, friends, son, in-laws,
everyone except the bosses he twisted

and wrung himself to please.
He was always hungry. If he ate five
sandwiches, his hunger still knocked
on his bones like a broken radiator
and he was never full.

He lived a hunger bigger than a man,
a hunger to be other, golden,
a hollowness finally now filled
with pain. He holds you in the phone
but his eyes seek the dark in the mirror.

He slips in and out of his deathbed
like a suit he keeps trying on, refitting.
He grabs at a hand and speaks the wrong
name, and the hand flops cold as a fish
while he calls till hoarseness, for himself.

The aunt I wanted to be

My aunt Ruth was the youngest girl,
halfway in age between my mother
and me. She read mysteries, so when
I was twelve and thirteen, I read all

the mysteries in Gabriel Richard
Library—where my favorite librarian
explained to me that the name whooshed,
being French, and rimed with hard.

I followed Ruth to the golf course,
carrying her clubs like bouquets
of exquisite flowers. I walked just
behind her, imitating her swinging walk.

How she laughed. It made me glad
to hear it building from her navel
and tumbling out. She was not
like my mother or other mothers.

She was childless and worked. She
earned her own money. She wore suits.
She wore slacks before other women
dared. She had rows of bowling

and golf trophies and muscles

she let me feel in her arm, but
her husband beat her. It was a
shame we never spoke aloud.

Sometimes she would wear makeup
so thick it flaked and still I could
see the purple rose on her cheek.
I did not love him. Nor did she.

She eloped with a neighbor, and off
they ran to California where they
were poor and merry and kept kosher
together and she gave up golf

for swimming and grew roses
and tomatoes. Behind every strong
woman my age someone like my aunt
stands like a signpost pointing:

to a place she could only glimpse
like Moses on Mt. Pisgah, that land
of freedom we promised ourselves
and are still fighting to conquer.

The flying Jew

I never met my uncle Dave.
The most real thing I know about him
is how he died, which he did
again and again in the middle of the night
my mother screaming, my father shouting,
Shut up, Bert, you're having a bad dream.

My uncle Dave, the recurring nightmare.
He was the Jew who flew.
How did he manage it? Flying was for
gentlemen, and he was a kid from the slums
of Philadelphia, Pittsburgh, Cleveland—
Zaydeh one headlong leap ahead of the law
and the Pinkertons, the goons who finally
bashed his head in when he was organizing
his last union, the bakery workers.

Dave looked up between the buildings,
higher than the filthy sparrows who pecked
at horse dung and the pigeons who strutted
and cooed in the tenement eaves,
up to the grey clouds of Philadelphia,
the rust clouds of Pittsburgh with the fires
of the open hearth steel mills staining them,
a pillar of smoke by day and fire by night.

He followed into the clouds.
My mother didn't even know who taught
him to fly, but he learned.
He became one with the plane, they said.
Off he went to France. He flew in combat,
was shot down and survived, never
became an ace, didn't enjoy combat,
the killing, but flying was better than sex.

He took my mother up once and she wept
the whole time. She wouldn't fly again
till she was seventy-five and said then
she didn't care if the plane went down.

It was his only talent, his only passion
and a good plane was a perfect fit for
his body and his mind, his reflexes.
The earth was something that clung to his shoes,
something to shake off, something to gather
all your strength into a taut charge
and then launch forward and leave behind.

After the war, he was lost for two years,
tried selling, tried insurance, then off
he went barnstorming with his war buddies.
Time on the ground was just stalling time,
killing time, parked in roominghouses

and tourist homes and bedbug hotels.
He drank little. Women were aspirin.

Being the only Jew, he had something
to prove every day, so he flew the fastest,
he did the final trick that made the audience
shriek. The planes grew older, the crowds
thinned out. One fall day outside Cleveland
he got his mother, sister Bert and her
little boy to watch the act. It was a triple
Immelmann roll he had done five hundred
shows but this time the plane plowed
into the earth and a fireball rose.

So every six months he died flaming
in the middle of the night, and all I
ever knew of him was Mother screaming.

My rich uncle, whom I only met three times

We were never invited to his house.
We went there once while they were all in Hawaii,
climbed steps from which someone had shoveled
the snow, not him, to the wide terrace.
Yellow brick, the house peered into fir and juniper.
It was too large for me to imagine what it held
but I was sure every one of them, four girls
and bony wife, each had a room of her own.

He had been a magician and on those rare
nights he had to stay at the Detroit Statler
downtown, he would summon us for supper
in the hotel restaurant. Mother would put on
and take off every dress in her closet, all six,
climb in the swaybacked brown Hudson muttering shame.
He would do tricks with his napkin and pull
quarters from my ears and spoons from his sleeves.

He had been a clumsy acrobat, he had failed at comedy
and vaudeville; he was entertaining for a party
when he met a widow with four girls and an inheritance.
He waltzed right out of her romantic movie dreams
and he strolled into her house and she had him redone.
He learned to talk almost like her dead husband.
He learned to wear suits, order dinners and give orders

to servants. His name changed, his background rebuilt,
his religion painted over, he almost fit in.

Of my uncles, only he was unreal, arriving by plane
to stay on the fanciest street in downtown Detroit.
The waiter brought a phone to the table, his broker
calling. I imagined a cowboy breaking horses.
He made knives disappear. He made a napkin vanish.
He was like an animated suit, no flesh, no emotions
bubbling the blood and steaming the windows as
my other uncles and aunts did. Only the discreet
Persian leather smell of money droned in my nose.

His longest trick was to render himself invisible.
Then one night after the guests had left, he went down
to the basement in the latest multi-level glass vast
whatnot shelf of house and hanged himself by the furnace.
They did not want his family at the funeral. She had
no idea, his wife said, why would he be depressed?
I remember his laugh like a cough and his varnished
face, buffed till the silverware shone in his eyes.
His last trick was to vanish himself forever.

A candle in a glass

When you died, it was time to light the first
candle of the eight. The dark tidal shifts
of the Jewish calendar of waters and the moon
that grows like a belly and starves like a rabbit
in winter have carried that holiday forward
and back since then. I light only your candle
at sunset, as the red wax of the sun melts
into the rumpled waters of the bay.

The ancient words pass like cold water
out of stone over my tongue as I say kaddish.
When I am silent and the twilight drifts
in on skeins of unraveling woolly snow
blowing over the hill dark with pitch pines,
I have a moment of missing that pierces
my brain like sugar stabbing a cavity
till the nerve lights its burning wire.

Grandmother Hannah comes to me at Pesach
and when I am lighting the sabbath candles.
The sweet wine in the cup has her breath.
The challah is braided like her long, long hair.
She smiles vaguely, nods, is gone like a savor
passing. You come oftener when I am putting

up pears or tomatoes, baking apple cake.
You are in my throat laughing or in my eyes.

When someone dies, it is the unspoken words
that spoil in the mind and ferment to wine
and to vinegar. I obey you still, going
out in the saw toothed wind to feed the birds
you protected. When I lie in the arms of my love,
I know how you climbed like a peavine twining,
lush, grasping for the sun, toward love
and always you were pinched back, denied.

It's a little low light the yahrtzeit candle
makes, you couldn't read by it or even warm
your hands. So the dead are with us only
as the scent of fresh coffee, of cinnamon,
of pansies excites the nose and then fades,
with us as the small candle burns in its glass.
We lose and we go on losing as long as we live,
a little winter no spring can melt.

Belly good

A heap of wheat, says the Song of Songs
but I've never seen wheat in a pile.
Apples, potatoes, cabbages, carrots
make lumpy stacks, but you are sleek
as a seal hauled out in the winter sun.

I can see you as a great goose egg
or a single juicy and fully ripe peach.
You swell like a natural grassy hill.
You are symmetrical as a Hopewell mound,
with the eye of the navel wide open,

the eye of my apple, the pear's port
window. You're not supposed to exist
at all this decade. You're to be flat
as a kitchen table, so children with
roller skates can speed over you

like those sidewalks of my childhood
that each gave a different roar under
my wheels. You're required to show
muscle striations like the ocean
sand at ebb tide, but brick hard.

Clothing is not designed for women
of whose warm and flagrant bodies

you are a swelling part. Yet I confess
I meditate with my hands folded on you,
a maternal cushion radiating comfort.

Even when I have been at my thinnest,
you have never abandoned me but curled
round as a sleeping cat under my skirt.
When I spread out, so do you. You like
to eat, drink and bang on another belly.

In anxiety I clutch you with nervous fingers
as if you were a purse full of calm.
In my grandmother standing in the fierce sun
I see your cauldron that held eleven children
shaped under the tent of her summer dress.

I see you in my mother at thirty
in her flapper gear, skinny legs
and then you knocking on the tight dress.
We hand you down like a prize feather quilt.
You are our female shame and sunburst strength.

The Chuppah

(MARRIAGE)

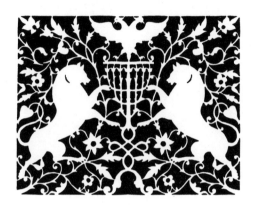

The chuppah

The chuppah stands on four poles.
The home has its four corners.
The chuppah stands on four poles.
The marriage stands on four legs.
Four points loose the winds
that blow on the walls of the house,
the south wind that brings the warm rain,
the east wind that brings the cold rain,
the north wind that brings the cold sun
and the snow, the long west wind
bringing the weather off the far plains.

Here we live open to the seasons.
Here the winds caress and cuff us
contrary and fierce as bears.
Here the winds are caught and snarling
in the pines, a cat in a net clawing
breaking twigs to fight loose.
Here the winds brush our faces
soft in the morning as feathers
that float down from a dove's breast.

Here the moon sails up out of the ocean
dripping like a just washed apple.
Here the sun wakes us like a baby.
Therefore the chuppah has no sides.

It is not a box.
It is not a coffin.

It is not a dead end.
Therefore the chuppah has no walls.
We have made a home together
open to the weather of our time.
We are mills that turn in the winds of struggle
converting fierce energy into bread.

The canopy is the cloth of our table
where we share fruit and vegetables
of our labor, where our care for the earth
comes back and we take its body in ours.

The canopy is the cover of our bed
where our bodies open their portals wide,
where we eat and drink the blood
of our love, where the skin shines red
as a swallowed sunrise and we burn
in one furnace of joy molten as steel
and the dream is flesh and flower.

O my love O my love we dance
under the chuppah standing over us
like an animal on its four legs,
like a table on which we set our love
as a feast, like a tent
under which we work
not safe but no longer solitary
in the searing heat of our time.

The wine

Red is the body's own deep song,
the color of lips, of our busy
organs, heart and stomach and lungs,
the color of our roused genitals,
the color of tongues and the flag of our blood.

Red is the loudest color
and the most secret
lurking inside the clothes' cocoon,
baked in the dark of the nightly bed
like coals shimmering in a stove.

It is the hot color, the active
that dances into your eye leaping,
that goads and pricks you
with its thorn of fire,
that shouts and urges and commands.

But red coils in the wineglass
head into tail like a dozing cat
whose eyes have shut but who purrs still
the pleasure of your hand, whose
warmth gently loosens the wine's aroma

so it rises like a perfumed ghost
inside the chambers of your nose.

In the mouth wine opens
its hundred petals like a damask rose
and then subsides, swallowed to afterglow.

In the wine press of the bed
of all the salty flows of our bodies,
the heat of our love ferments
our roundness into the midnight red
flowering of the wine

that can make drunken and make warm
that can comfort and quicken the sluggish
that can ease the weary body into sleep
that can frame the dark bread and cheese
into feast, that can celebrate

and sing through the wine of the body,
its own bright blood that rushes
to every cranny and cove of the flesh
and dark of the bone, the joy in love
that is the wine of life.

House built of breath

Words plain as pancakes syruped with endearment.
Simple as potatoes, homely as cottage cheese.

Wet as onions, dry as salt.
Slow as honey, fast as seltzer,

my raisin, my sultana, my apricot love
my artichoke, furry one, my pineapple

I love you daily as milk,
I love you nightly as aromatic port.

The words trail a bitter slime like slugs,
then in the belly warm like cabbage borscht.

The words are hung out on the line,
sheets for the wind to bleach.

The words are simmering slowly
on the back burner like a good stew.

Words are the kindling in the wood stove.
Even the quilt at night is stuffed with word down.

When we are alone the walls sing
and even the cats talk but only in Yiddish.

When we are alone we make love in deeds.
And then in words. And then in food.

Nailing up the mezuzah

A friend from Greece
brought a tin house
on a plaque, designed
to protect our abode,
as in Greek churches
embossed legs or hearts
on display entreat aid.
I hung it but now
nail my own proper charm.

I refuse no offers of help,
at least from friends,
yet this presence
is long overdue. Mostly
we nurture our own
blessings or spoil them,
build firmly or undermine
our walls. Who are termites
but our obsessions gnawing?

Still the winds blow hard
from the cave of the sea
carrying off what they will.
Our smaller luck abides
like a worm snug in an apple
who does not comprehend
the shivering of the leaves
as the ax bites hard
in the smooth trunk.

We need all help proffered
by benign forces. Outside
we commit our beans to the earth,
the tomato plants started
in February to the care
of the rain. My little
pregnant grey cat offers
the taut bow of her belly
to the sun's hot tongue.

Saturday I watched alewives
swarm in their thousands
waiting in queues quivering
pointed against the white
rush of the torrents
to try their leaps upstream.
The gulls bald as coffin
nails stabbed them casually
conversing in shrieks, picnicking.

On its earth, this house
is oriented. We grow
from our bed rooted firmly
as an old willow into the water
of our dreams flowing deep
in the hillside. This hill
is my temple, my soul.
Malach ha-moves, angel of death
pass over, pass on.

In the grip of the solstice

Feels like a train roaring into night,
the journey into fierce cold just beginning.
The ground is newly frozen, the crust
brittle and fancy with striations,
steeples and nipples we break
under our feet.

Every day we are shortchanged a bit more,
night pressing down on the afternoon
throttling it. Wan sunrise later
and later, every day trimmed
like an old candle you beg to give
an hour's more light.

Feels like hurtling into vast darkness,
the sky itself whistling of space
the black matter between stars
the red shift as the light dies,
warmth a temporary aberration,
entropy as a season.

Our ancestors understood the brute
fear that grips us as the cold
settles around us, closing in.

Light the logs in the fireplace tonight,
light the candles, first one, then two,
the full chanukiya.

Light the fire in the belly.
Eat hot soup, cabbage and beef
borscht, chicken soup, lamb
and barley, stoke the marrow.
Put down the white wine and pour
whiskey instead.

We reach for each other in our bed,
the night vaulted above us
like a cave. Night in the afternoon,
cold frosting the glass so it hurts
to touch it, only flesh still
welcoming to flesh.

The real hearth

Let's heat up the night to a boil.
Let's cook every drop of liquid
out of our flesh till we sizzle,
not a drop of come left.

We are pots on too high a flame.
Our insides char and flake
dark like sinister snow idling down.
We breathe out smoke.

We die out and sleep covers
us in ashes. We lie without
dreaming, empty as clean grates.
Only breath moves hissing.

Yet we wake rebuilt, clattering
and hungry as waterfalls leaping off,
rushing into the day, roaring
our bright intentions.

It is the old riddle in the Yiddish
song, what can burn and not burn up,
a heart, a body, passion that gives
birth to itself every day.

The body does not wear out with
use, nor does love, so let us
use each other in the best of ways
as the hours jump off the cliff.

All lovers have secret names

The day I forget to write
the day I forget to feed the cats
the day I forget to love you
the day I forget your name
and then my own.

Until then I will not cease
this spinning pattern: part weave
of skeins of soft wool to keep
us warm, to clothe our too open
flesh, to decorate us—

and part dance, through woods
where roots trip me, a dance
through meadows of rabbit holes
and old ribs of plowing hidden
under thick grass.

Until then I will whirl
through my ragged days.
Like a spindle, like a dreydl
I will turn in the center
of my intricate weave

spelling your name in my dance
in my weaving, in my work,
your hidden name which
is simply, finally,
love.

Marriage in winter

What we need is to focus sharply.
What we need is to attack the wind.
What we need is to grab each other
as if we were a rope thrown
into a pit.

The pit exists.
The pit surrounds us each alone.
Our hearts are pitted like the stony
surface of the moon, cratered
and bitter cold.

What we need is to thrust
into each other with a hunger
for spring, the bear in each
wakened from hibernation
lean and toothy and fast.

We are starving for love
in the midst of love: we
are fans churning the dirty
air, pumping our own exhaust.
We waste ourselves to noise.

How shall we open our doors
and windows wide to each other?

How shall we come dancing
in the twilight under a rain
of apple blossoms, a weekly
shabbat wedding made new?

We must touch each other with
wonder, kiss with hunger.
We must enter each other
as if we were a new garden
strange and fruitful and fragrant
with vines and trees
we have dreamed but never seen.

Tikkun Olam

(REPAIR OF THE WORLD)

תקון עולם

The ark of consequence

The classic rainbow shows as an arc,
a bridge strung in thinning clouds,
but I have seen it flash a perfect circle,
rising and falling and rising again
through the octave of colors,
a sun shape rolling like a wheel of light.

Commonly it is a fraction of a circle,
a promise only partial, not a banal
sign of safety like a smile pin,
that rainbow cartoon affixed to vans
and baby carriages. No, it promises
only, this world will not self-destruct.

Account the rainbow a boomerang of liquid
light, foretelling rather that what we
toss out returns in the water table;
flows from the faucet into our bones.
What we shoot up into orbit falls
to earth one night through the roof.

Think of it as a promise that what
we do continues in an arc
of consequence, flickers in our
children's genes, collects in each

spine and liver, gleams in the apple,
coats the down of the drowning auk.

When you see the rainbow iridescence
shiver in the oil slick, smeared
on the waves of the poisoned river,
shudder for the covenant broken, for we
are given only this floating round ark
with the dead moon for company and warning.

To be of use

The people I love the best
jump into work head first
without dallying in the shallows
and swim off with sure strokes almost out of sight.
They seem to become natives of that element,
the black sleek heads of seals
bouncing like half-submerged balls.

I love people who harness themselves, an ox to a heavy
  cart,
who pull like water buffalo, with massive patience,
who strain in the mud and the muck to move things
  forward,
who do what has to be done, again and again.

I want to be with people who submerge
in the task, who go into the fields to harvest
and work in a row and pass the bags along,
who are not parlor generals and field deserters
but move in a common rhythm
when the food must come in or the fire be put out.

The work of the world is common as mud.
Botched, it smears the hands, crumbles to dust.
But the thing worth doing well done

has a shape that satisfies, clean and evident.
Greek amphoras for wine or oil,
Hopi vases that held corn, are put in museums
but you know they were made to be used.
The pitcher cries for water to carry
and a person for work that is real.

Available light

Ripe and runny as perfect Brie, at this age
appetites mature rampant and allowed.
I am wet as a salt marsh under the flood tide
of the full solstice moon and dry as salt itself
that draws the superfluous juice from the tissues
to leave the desiccated butterfly wing intact.

I know myself as I know the four miles I walk
every morning, the sky like ice formed on skim
milk, the sky dappled and fat and rolling, never
the same two hours later. I know there are rooms
upon caverns opening off corridors I will never
enter, as well as those I'll be thrust into.

I am six with my mother watching clippers
take off for Lisbon. I am nine and the President
whose voice is a personal god is dying in the radio.
I am twelve and coming while I mutter yes, yes,
of course, this is what the bones grow around to hold.
I am twenty-four as my best friend bleeds her life out.

At any moment I find myself under the water of my
past trying to breathe in that thick refracted medium.
At any moment a new voice is speaking me like a p.a.
system that one day amplifies a lecture on newts

and the next day jazz. I am always finding new
beings in me like otters swimming in the soup.

I have friends who gave themselves to Marx, to Freud,
to A.A., to Christianity or Buddhism or Goddess
religions, to the Party or the Lord or the Lover.
As a Jew, I have a god who returns me to myself
uncleaned, to be used again, since forgiveness must
be made but changes not one needle falling from the pine.

As consequences show their lengthened teeth
from the receding gums, we hunger for the larger
picture, the longer view, and yet and yet
I cannot augment the natural curve of earth
except by including the moth and the mammoth,
the dark river percolating through the sea

built rock, the dense memories of shell
and sediment, the million deaths recorded
in each inch; the warm funky breath
of Leviathan as he breached off the portside;
people in boots struggling to shove the pilot
whales free that a storm surge grounded.

In winter the light is red and short.
The sun hangs its wizened rosehip in the oaks.
By midafternoon night is folding in.
The ground is locked against us like a door.

Yet faces shine so the eyes stretch for them
and tracks in the snow are etched, calligraphy

I learn by rote and observation, patient
the way I am finally learning Hebrew
at fifty, forgiving my dead parents
who saw squinting by their own scanty light.
By four o'clock I must give up the woods,
come in, turn on every lamp to read.

Later when the moon has set I go out
and let the spears of Sirius and Rigel
pierce the ivory of my skull and enter
my blood like glowing isotopes of distance.
I stand in the cold vault of the night
and see more and fainter stars as my eyes

clear or my blood cools. The barred owl
hoots. The skunk prances past me to stir
the compost pile with her sharp nails.
A lithe weasel flicks across the cul de sac.
Even the dead of winter: it seethes with more
than I can ever live to name and speak.

For she is a tree of life

In the cramped living room of my childhood
between sagging rough-skinned sofa that made me itch
and swaybacked chair surrounded by ashtrays
where my father read every word of the paper
shrouded in blue smoke, coughing rusty phlegm
and muttering doom, the rug was a factory
oriental and the pattern called tree of life.

My mother explained as we plucked a chicken,
tree of life: I was enthralled and Hannah
my grandmother hummed for me the phrase
from liturgy: Eytz khayim hee l'makhazikim
bo v'kol nitee-voteh-ho shalom:
for she is a tree of life to all who hold her fast,
and the fruit of her branches is peace.

I see her big bosomed and tall as a maple
and in her veins the beige sugar of desire
running sometimes hard, surging skyward
and sometimes sunk down into the roots
that burrow and wriggle deep and far among rocks
and clay and the bones of rabbits and foxes
lying in the same bed at last becoming one.

I see her opening into flushed white
blossoms the bees crawl into. I see her

branches dipping under the weight of the yield,
the crimson, the yellow and russet globes,
apples fallen beneath the deer crunch.
Yellow jackets in the cobalt afternoon buzz
drunken from cracked fruit oozing juice.

We all flit through her branches or creep
through her bark, skitter over her leaves.
Yet we are the mice that gnaw at her root
who labor ceaselessly to bring her down.
When the tree falls, we will not rise as plastic
butterfly spaceships, but will starve as the skies
weep hot acid and the earth chafes into dust.

One bird, if there is only one, dies in the night

I dropped my spoon into my yogurt
at the crack of bird against window.
I ran in sneakers into the snow.

Often their spleens rupture
or their necks break. This one
was tiny, stunned. The wind

had fangs. Ice formed in my
lungs as I picked it up.
I put on my coat over it and walked.

It woke up slowly, turning to stare.
It clutched my finger by reflex
after an hour. Nearby I could hear

the sheer cries of its partners,
little panes of ice breaking.
I identified it at leisure, bird

in my hand, Peterson's open.
A golden crowned kinglet, so those cries
were stitches that bound them together,

birds the size of a hen's egg
who must clutch each other all night

to survive winters, so they call

all day, where are you? Here
I am, here. Finally it beat its wings
panicstricken after two intimate hours.

How often I feel I need a certain
number of companions or possible allies
to survive, say passing through Utah

or South Carolina. I count women
in a crowd, guess at Jews, feminists,
lefties, writers, all those we count

as someone who might watch our backside
so it won't fall off, who might
warm us through a lethal night's freeze.

Yahrtzeit

Everything I have written about
has shriveled into black marks
on paper, everything real I mean
blood into ink.

I remember my dead as if
through dirty water. Once
you walked through me
and your faces were knives.

Your voices summoned me
from sleep like something falling,
a tree limb slamming into
the house, the window broken,

rain puddled on the floor,
soaking the covers. Now
you are a chill on the back
of my hands for an instant.

Pain abates into a bruise
barely visible. Soon gone.
Yet sometimes memory cracks
open like a silver egg

and you emerge with your
hawk's eyes glaring
and you stab straight for my heart
and it stops.

After the wind abated,
he walked out and died

for Arne Manos (1941–1991)

A little green snake trapped
like a silken braid
in the hands, quick jerk
of the supple spine
and it glides free
gone into the camouflage grass.

Blue eyes of the dayflower
weed among the alyssum
like the hemerocallis
opens each day its fresh flower
that fades and withers
with the bleeding sun.

I would have eaten more chocolate
if I'd known, said the dying
woman, I would have told all
my affection, I would have lain
reading the worry beads of his spine
an hour to each.

But we do know.
The clock face opens and
closes its scissor hands

cutting us from the minute
the hour that never
comes back.

The watch in our chest keeps
time for us—keeps? No,
spends the time as it runs through
us on its millipede legs.
This is our longest dance, but we
lose the patterns we are casting.

We die always in the moment
like a book falling shut
and the story is finished except
for those resonances that darken
in the minds of others, toward silence
and the long cold between the stars.

Woman in a shoe

There was an old woman who lived
in a shoe, her own two shoes,
men's they were, brown and worn.
They flapped when she hobbled along.

There was an old woman who lived
in a refrigerator box, under
the expressway, with her cat.
January, they died curled together.

There was an old woman who lived
in a room under the roof. It
got hot, but she was scared
to open the window. It got hotter.

Too hot, too cold, too poor,
too old. Invisible unless
she annoys you, invisible
unless she gets in your way.

In fairy tales if you are kind
to an old woman, she gives you
the thing you desperately need:
an unconquerable sword, a purse

bottomless and always filled,
a magical ring. We don't believe

that anymore. Such tales were
made up by old women scared

to be thrust from the hearth,
shoved into the street to starve.
Who fears an old woman pushing
a grocery cart? She is talking

to God as she shuffles along,
her life in her pockets. You
are the true child of her heart
and you see living garbage.

Up and out

1. *The foot gnawed off*

We occupy neighborhoods like roominghouses.
The Irish lived here; the Italians, then the Jews,
then the Blacks up from the South and now
the Vietnamese fill this dirty decaying motel.
Nobody imagines staying. Success means getting out.

To be in a place then is only a move in a game;
who can love a box on a board? Remaining
is being stuck. My parents amused themselves
all through my childhood by choosing houses
from the Sunday paper to visit.

They could not afford to buy but pretended.
They wanted to walk through the large rooms
of their fantasies criticizing the wallpaper,
counting other people's chairs, imagining
waking in that bedroom on that street.

How can we belong to ourselves, when home
is something to pry yourself out of
like a pickup stuck on a sand road;
when what holds you has to be sacrificed
as a fox will gnaw off a foot to be free.

Growing up, what you love most can trap you.
Friends are for discarding. Lovers

for saying goodbye. Marriage looks like a closet.
Even your faithful dog could slow you down.
Polish your loneliness until its headlight shines.

Always what formed you, those faces
that hung like ripe apples in the tree
of your childhood: the hands that caressed you,
whose furtive touch untied the knot of pleasure
and loosened your flesh till it fluttered

and streamed with joy; those who taught you
fear at the end of a bright knife; who taught
you patience as their lips fumbled to force into
sounds strange squiggles blurring on the page;
who taught you guile as the hand teases the eye

into illusion; who gave you the names you really
use for the parts of your body, for the rush
of your anger hard into your teeth and fists;
always what formed you will come trailing guilt
like a cloud of fine ashes from burnt hair.

You will always be struck into memory like a match
spurting and then burn out in silence, because
there is no one to say, yes, I too remember,
I know how it was. We litter our past
on the sides of roads in fast food wrappers.

2. Soft coal country

We used to drive to Ebensburg in the soft coal
country of Pennsylvania, an old brick Victorian
on the bottom of High Street where trucks shifted gears
to start their descent or labored upward all night;
from the backbone of High the ribs of side streets
like a fish carcass fell sharply away into gullies.
Around it were the miners' towns it served,
the grim company towns with the made-up names, Revloc,
Colver; the miners' shanties clinging to the sides
of hogback ridges, Nantiglo, Monday's Corners.

All the roads were blasted through rock.
On Horseshoe Curve you could watch the long long
freights toiling up and shrieking down, miles
around the crescent. The mountains had an anger
in them. The stone oozed bright water stained
with iron. I muttered the names of towns like prayers
returning with my father because a man must visit
his family. This was a place he had to leave,
so afraid of ending up with all Grandmother's Lloyds
grubbing in the mines that when they shone
their sweet smiles at weddings, funerals, he'd
pretend he could not tell cousin from cousin.

Later when the mines shut and all the first
and second cousins were out of work for the fifth
year running and their families cracking along

old troubles, where they'd been glued, he said,
See, you can't make an honest living here.

I loved the mountains; he merely conquered them.
He returned not to see but to be seen, wearing
his one good suit, driving his nearly new car,
showing off the sexy black-haired wife not like any
in his high school yearbook, although they all knew
to sniff and say, Jew. Always the morning we left
he was up an hour early, tapping his foot under
the table, lighting cigarette from half-smoked butt
and then he would stomp his foot on the accelerator
and take the mountain roads clocking himself against
some pursuing maw so that if he did not push the car
and himself to the edge of danger, he would be back,
back with his desperate nagging sisters counting pennies
with a mountain on his chest pinning him down.

3. When I was caddy

Cleveland was the promised land of my childhood,
where my bubba cooked kosher and even her cat had good
manners and sat at the table, and she told me that
when they were alone, he used a knife and fork.
I always hoped he would do it while I was eating.

I remember the smell of the women when I pressed
against her side behind the mehitzah, camphor,

eucalyptus, cinnamon, lavender, sweat. Aunt Ruth
was the smartest girl, closer in age to me
than to my mother. When I was ten she married

into the middle class and took Grandma to the suburbs.
She worked for the Navy. What a pity you don't
have a degree, they were always telling her,
but she did the work without a rating. Driven
to excel, she began to replace all the bowling

trophies with golfing trophies. We walked to
the course through the flat green morning swishing
with sprinklers, both of us almost tiptoeing. It was
so clean and neat, the streets like a funeral parlor
full of gladiolus, we tried to talk softly, properly.

All Grandma's cronies were back in the ghetto.
There was no synagogue for miles. No kosher butcher.
She ate a lot of canned salmon and packaged soup.
Without neighbors to gossip about important things
she turned to the soaps and worried about Helen Trent.

Suddenly my mother was taking phone calls at one a.m.
She was warning, Do you want to lose it all?
So he hit you. So what else is new to wives?
Then Grandma and Ruth were back in the ghetto,
now partly Black, and Grandma was cooking again.

The kitchen smelled the way it should and so did she.
Old ladies were drinking tea in glasses and quoting

Lenin and their own rabbis. Every strike was fought over.
Every young woman's reputation was put through a sieve.
Every grandchild was taken and properly raised.

And me, I was back, oh briefly, briefly back
in the promised land of love and endless stories
before cancer ate Grandma, savoring each organ
but leaving her voice till the end. And Aunt Ruth
ran till she came to the Pacific and then fell down.

4. *Toward a good rooting medium*

The Ojibwa said to me, My people have lived
on this sea since the mountains moved.
(The last ice age.) Our heart is here.
When we move to the cities, we blow into dust.

There are villages in Cornwall
continuously occupied for five thousand years.
Jericho has been a city since 7000 B.C.E.
I've known families who farmed their soil

and gave their bones to it till it was as known
to them as the face of a mother or the body
of one passionately loved; people who have come back
to the same place year after year, and retired on it,

walking its seasons till they can read the sky
like a personal letter; fishermen who could taste

a stream and tell you what the trout were doing.
This is not a pastoral: once I loved Manhattan so.

A friend could walk Paris streets on a map, sketching
the precise light, the houses, the traffic sounds.
Perhaps we should practice by loving a lilac bush.
Practice on a brick, an oriole nest, a tire of petunias.

O home over the expressway under a sky like something
you step in and scrape off your boot, heaped
ashtray we are stubbed into with smouldering butts,
billboards touting cancer under the carbolic rain!

Will the Lenni-Lenape take back New Jersey?
The fish glow in the dark thrashing in dying
piles on every chenille bedspread, a light by which
we can almost read the fine print on the ceiling.

Love it because you can't leave it. Love it
or kill it. What we throw away returns in the blood
and leaves a chemical stain on the cell walls.
Huck honey, there's no territory to light out to.

That glow is from refineries on the farther shore.
Take your trash out with you or hunker down.
This is the Last Chance Saloon and Health Spa.
In heaven as on earth the dishes must be done.

The task never completed

No task is ever completed,
only abandoned or pressed into use.
Tinkering can be a form of prayer.

Twenty-six botched worlds preceded
Genesis we are told in ancient commentary,
and ha-Shem said not only,

of this particular attempt,
It is good, but muttered,
if only it will hold.

Incomplete, becoming, the world
was given us to fix, to complete
and we've almost worn it out.

My house was hastily built,
on the cheap. Leaks, rotting
sills, the floor a relief map of Idaho.

Whenever I get some money, I stove
up, repair, add on, replace.
This improvisation permits me to squat

here on the land that owns me.
We evolve through mistakes, wrong

genes, imitation gone wild.

Each night sleep unravels me into wool,
then into sheep and wolf. Walls and fire
pass through me. I birth stones.

Every dawn I stumble from the roaring
vat of dreams and make myself up
remembering and forgetting by halves.

Every dawn I choose to take a knife
to the world's flank or a sewing kit,
rough improvisation, but a start.

Toldot, Midrashim

(OF HISTORY AND INTERPRETATION)

תולדות מדרשים

Apple sauce for Eve

Those old daddies cursed you and us in you,
damned for your curiosity: for your sin
was wanting knowledge. To try, to taste,
to take into the body, into the brain
and turn each thing, each sign, each factoid
round and round as new facets glint and white
fractures into colors and the image breaks
into crystal fragments that pierce the nerves
while the brain casts the chips into patterns.

Each experiment sticks a finger deep in the pie,
dares existence, blows a horn in the ear
of belief, lets the nasty and difficult brats
of real questions into the still air
of the desiccated parlor of stasis.
What we all know to be true, constant,
melts like frost landscapes on a window
in a jet of steam. How many last words
in how many dead languages would translate into,
But what happens if I, and Whoops!

We see Adam wagging his tail, good dog, good
dog, while you and the snake shimmy up the tree,
lab partners in a dance of will and hunger,
that thirst not of the flesh but of the brain.
Men always think women are wanting sex,

cock, snake, when it is the world she's after.
The birth trauma for the first conceived kid
of the ego, I think therefore I am, I
kick the tree, who am I, why am I,
going, going to die, die, die.

You are indeed the mother of invention,
the first scientist. Your name means
life: finite, dynamic, swimming against
the current of time, tasting, testing,
eating knowledge like any other nutrient.
We are all the children of your bright hunger.
We are all products of that first experiment,
for if death was the worm in that apple,
the seeds were freedom and the flowering of choice.

The Book of Ruth and Naomi

When you pick up the Tanakh and read
the Book of Ruth, it is a shock
how little it resembles memory.
It's concerned with inheritance,
lands, men's names, how women
must wiggle and wobble to live.

Yet women have kept it dear
for the beloved elder who
cherished Ruth, more friend than
daughter. Daughters leave. Ruth
brought even the baby she made
with Boaz home as a gift.

Where you go, I will go too,
your people shall be my people,
I will be a Jew for you,
for what is yours I will love
as I love you, oh Naomi
my mother, my sister, my heart.

Show me a woman who does not dream
a double, heart's twin, a sister
of the mind in whose ear she can whisper,
whose hair she can braid as her life

twists its pleasure and pain and shame.
Show me a woman who does not hide

in the locket of bone that deep
eye beam of fiercely gentle love
she had once from mother, daughter,
sister; once like a warm moon
that radiance aligned the tides
of her blood into potent order.

At the season of first fruits we recall
two travelers, co-conspirators, scavengers
making do with leftovers and mill ends,
whose friendship was stronger than fear,
stronger than hunger, who walked together
the road of shards, hands joined.

Fathers and sons

Abraham laboring for dominion and increase
came to the rich moist land of grasses
after walking the desert of cackling sky
where the sun beat on stone gongs
dry as his throat, his palms, his eyes.
Abraham laboring to satisfaction and increase
worked the valleys and subjugated the hills,
sent the unclean into exile,
saw his worth grow with the seasons
and in winter begot a son.
His son increased
who had never drunk sheep piss for thirst,
who had never seen his hard-tried men and flocks
fall shrunken on the stones.
His son sat up all night with friends
discussing how he would redistribute the land,
make peace with small dark hill people
who used stone axes and died slowly.
When the challenge came
Abraham met it with his best.
He did not allow opportunity for debate
though while the knife was at the boy's throat
he made a short heartfelt speech
about dedication.

At the well

Though I'm blind now and age
has gutted me to rubbing bones
knotted up in a leather sack
like Old Man Jacob I wrestled an angel.
It happened near that well by Peniel
where the water runs copper cold
even in drought. Sore and dusty
I was traveling my usual rounds
wary of strangers, for some men
think nothing of setting on any woman
alone, doctoring a bit, setting bones,
herbs and simples I know well,
divining for water with a switch,
selling my charms of odd shaped bones
and stones with fancy names to less
skeptical women wanting a lover, a son,
a husband, or relief from one.

The stones were sharp as shinbones under me.
When I woke up at midnight it had come,
not he, I thought, not she but a presence furious
as a goat about to butt.
Amused as those yellow eyes
sometimes seem just before the hind
legs kick hard.
The angel struck me
and we wrestled all that night.
My dust stained gristle of a body
clad in proper village black
was pushed against him

and his fiery chest
fell through me like a star.
Raw with bruises, with my muscles
sawing like donkey's brays,
I thought fighting can be
making love. Then in the grey
placental dawn I saw.

"I know you now, face
on a tree of fire
with eyes of my youngest sweetest
dead, face
I saw in the mirror
right after my first child
was born—before it failed—
when I was beautiful.
Whatever you are, whatever
I've won a blessing
from you. Bless me!"

The angel, "Yes, we have met
at doors thrust open to an empty room,
a garden, or a pit.
My gifts have human faces
hieroglyphs that command
you without yielding what they mean.
Cast yourself
and I will bless your cast
till your bones are dice
for the wind to roll.

I am the demon of beginnings
for those who leap their thresholds
and let the doors swing shut."

My hair bristling, I stood.
"Get away from me, old
enemy. I know the lying
radiance of that face:
my friend, my twin, my
lover I trusted as the fish
the water, who left me
carrying his child.
The man who bought me
with his strength and beat
me for his weakness.
The girl I saved who turned
and sold her skin
for an easy bed in a house
of slaves. The boy fresh
as a willow sapling
smashed on the stones of war."

"I am the spirit of hinges,
the fever that lives in dice
and cards, what is picked
up and thrown down. I am
the new that is ancient,
the hope that hurts,
what begins in what has ended.
Mine is the double vision

that everything is sacred, and trivial,
the laughter that bubbles in blood,
and I love the blue beetle
clicking in the grass as much
as you. Shall I bless you,
child and crone?"

"What has plucked the glossy
pride of hair from my scalp,
loosened my teeth in their sockets,
wrung my breasts dry as gullies,
rubbed ashes into my sleep
but chasing you?
Now I clutch a crust and I hold on.
Get from me
wielder of the heart's mirages.
I will follow you to no more graves."

I spat
and she gathered her tall shuddering wings
and scaled the streaks of the dawn
a hawk on fire soaring
and I stood there and could hear the water burbling
and raised my hand
before my face and groped:
Why has the sun gone out?
Why is it dark?

Growing up haunted

When I enter through the hatch of memory
those claustrophobic chambers,
my adolescence in the booming fifties
of General Eisenhower, General Foods
and General Motors, I see our dreams:
obsolescent mannequins in Dior frocks
armored, prefabricated bodies;
and I see our nightmares, powerful
as a wine red sky and wall of fire.

Fear was the underside of every leaf
we turned, the knowledge that our
cousins, our other selves, had been
starved and butchered to ghosts.
The question every smoggy morning
presented like a covered dish:
why are you living and all those
mirror selves, sisters, gone
into smoke like stolen cigarettes?

I remember my grandmother's cry
when she learned the death of all she
remembered, girls she bathed with,
young men with whom she shyly
flirted, wooden shul where
her father rocked and prayed,

red haired aunt plucking the
balalaika, world of sun and snow
turned to shadows on a yellow page.

Assume no future you may not have
to fight for, to die for, muttered
ghosts gathered on the foot
of my bed each night. What you
carry in your blood is us,
the books we did not write,
music we could not make, a world
gone from gristle to smoke, only
as real now as words can make it.

The thief

Dina sent me a postcard,
history at a glance,
Sonka of the golden hand,
the notorious thief
being put in chains.

She looks young still, dark hair,
unsmiling—why would she?
1915, surrounded by Russian men
two blacksmiths preparing
the chains and three soldiers
to guard her, weaponless.

A Jew from Odessa, she could
move faster than water
as quiet as a leaf growing
more lightly than a shaft
of sun tapping your arm.

Like all young women
she was full of desires
little hot pomegranate seeds
bursting in her womb,

wishes crying from the dull
mirror of poverty.

Sonka heard the voices calling
from inside the coins,
take me, Sonka, take me
turn me into something sweet
turn me into something warm and soft
a cashmere shawl, a silk mantilla
a coat of fur like a bed of loving.

Eat me, said the chicken.
Drink me, the brandy sang.
Wear me, the blouse whispered.

Sonka of the golden hands
stands in the grim yard
of the prison, with her quick
hands bound in iron bracelets
calling with her solemn eyes:

Let me go, oh you who stare
at me and jail me in your
camera, now at last
free me to dance again
as I freed
those captured coins.

For each age, its amulet

Each illness has its demon, burning you with
its fever, beating its quick wings.
Do not leave an infant alone in the house,
my grandmother said, for Lilith is hovering,
hungry. Avoid sleeping in a new house alone.
Demons come to death as flies do, hanging
on the sour sweetish wind. Protect yourself
in an unclean place by spitting three times.
A pregnant woman must go to bed with a knife.
Put iron in a hen's nest to keep it laying.
Demons suck eggs and squeeze the breath from chicks.
Circle yourself with salt and pray.

By building containers of plutonium
with the power to kill for longer than humans
have walked upright, demons are driven off.
Demons lurk in dark skins, white skins,
demons speak another language, have funny hair.
Very fast planes that fall from the sky
regularly like ostriches trying to fly, protect.
Best of all is the burning of money ritually
in the pentagon shaped shrine. In Langley
the largest prayer wheel computer recites spells
composed of all words written, spoken, thought
taped and stolen from every living person.

The Altneushul in the old Prague ghetto

Craggy lines stoop against a crowded sky,
pastel candy boxes of flats pressing in,
built after the ghetto was bulldozed
in haste, memory wiped by imitation luxury,
as neighborhoods in my country are torn down
for condos and high rise cabinets.

Yet they left a few architectural jewels:
town hall with its backwards running clock,
the Pinkus Synagogue in one corner of a cemetery
crowded as rush hour—a building Spanish
in nostalgia; on its walls the names etched
of thousands harvested by Hitler.

Outside, the Altneushul seems gnarled,
kneeling. One wall is a menorah of bricks.
You go down to go in, into the earth
like a corpse, through a dark long anteroom.
The holy space is austere, vertical.
Through slits of windows, light slides in.

I call this austere, though every object
is dense with detail, because the eye
glides past them to the stark cliffs
of white that stand up majestic, simple

as rock. These walls have a deep resonance
that sets your bones wailing like an organ.

It says first go down in the body's earth
and smell the wet wormy clay, darkness
like fog that clings to your skin. Then let
your eyes scale the white walls as the first
sun enters the eastern window and prayer begins.
Here you slam against fact and then rejoice.

Returning to the cemetery
in the old Prague ghetto

Like bad teeth jammed crooked in a mouth
I think, no, because it goes on and on,
rippling over uneven hillocks among the linden
trees drooping, their papery leaves piling
up in the narrow paths that thread
between the crowded tilting slabs.

Stone pages the wind blew open.
The wind petrified into individual
cries. Prisoners penned together
with barely room to stand upright.
Souls of the dead Jews of Prague
waiting for justice under the acid rain.

So much and no further shall you go,
your contaminated dead confined between
strait walls like the ghetto itself.
So what to do? Every couple of generations,
pile on the dirt, raise the stones up
and add another layer of fresh bones.

The image I circle and do not want:
naked pallid bodies whipped through
the snow and driven into the chamber,

so crowded that dying slowly in the poison
cloud they could not fall as their nerves
burned slowly black, upright in death.

In my luggage I carried from Newcomb Hollow
two stones for Rabbi Loew's memorial
shaped like a narrow tent, one for Judah
on his side and one for Perl on hers.
But my real gift is the novel they
speak through. For David Gans, astronomer,

geographer, historian, insatiably curious
and neat as a cat in his queries,
I brought a fossil to lay at the foot
of his grave marked with a goose and a star,
Mogen David, so the illiterate could find
him, as Judah has his rampant lion.

In sixty-eight I had to be hoisted
over the fence. Among the stones
I was alone except for a stray black cat
that sang to me incessantly of need,
so hungry it ate bread from my jacket pocket.
This year buses belch out German tourists

and the graves are well tended.
This is a place history clutches you
by the foot as you walk the human earth,

like a hand grabbing from the grave,
not to frighten but to admonish.
Remember. History is the iron

in your blood carrying oxygen
so you can burn food and live.
Read this carved book with your fingers
and your failing eyes. The language
will speak in you silently
nights afterward, stone and bone.

The housing project at Drancy

Trains without signs flee through Paris.
Wrong trains. The wrong station.
The world as microwave oven, burning from within.
We arrive. Drancy looks like Inkster,
Gary, the farther reaches of Newark.

In the station they won't give directions.
C'est pas notre affaire. We don't deal with that.
Outside five buses limp in five directions
into the hot plain drugged with exhaust.
Nobody ever heard of the camp. They turn away.

Out on the bridge, over marshaling yards:
Here Jews were stuffed into cars nailed shut.
Here children too young to know their names
were counted like so many shoes
as they begged the French police hemming them in,

Take me to the bathroom, please, please,
before I wet myself. Mother, I have been so good,
and it is so very dark. Dear concierge,
I am writing to you as everyone else
is dead now and they are taking me away.

Yes, to the land children named Pitchepois,
giant's skull land grimmer than Hansel came to.

On the bridge I saw an old bald workman
staring down and I told myself desperately,
He is a communist and will answer me.

I asked him where the camp was, now a housing
project. He asked, Why do you want to know?
I had that one ready. No talk of novels, research.
My aunt was there. Oh, in that case,
he pointed to distant towers. You want that bus.

Where we descended the bus, Never heard of it.
Eyes that won't look. Then a woman asked that
same question, Why do you want to know?
A housing project crammed with mothers.
The guard towers are torn down and lindens grow.

In flats now with heat and plumbing, not eighty
but one family lives. Pain still rises,
the groaning of machinery deep underfoot.
Crimes ignored sink into the soil like PCBs
and enter the bones of children.

Black Mountain

On Montagne Noire creeping everywhere under the
    beech trees
were immense black slugs the size and pattern
of blown truck tires exploded by the superhighway.
Diamonds patterned their glossy and glittering backs.

As we watched, leaves, whole flowers disappeared in
    three bites.
Such avidity rebuked our stomachs skittish with alien
water and strange food. In patches of sunlight filtered
down, the slugs shone like wet black glass.

Battlefields are like any other fields; a forest
where men and women fought tanks with Sten guns
houses as many owl and rabbit and deer as the next hill
where nothing's happened since the Romans passed by.

Yet I have come without hesitation through the maze
of lumbering roads to this spot where the small marker
tells us we have reached a destination. To die here
under hemlock's dark drooping boughs, better I think

than shoved into the showers of gas to croak like roaches
too packed in to flail in the intense slow pain
as the minutes like lava cooling petrified the jammed
bodies into living rock, basalt pillars whose fingers

gouged grooves in cement. Yes, better to drop in the high
clean air and let your blood soak into the rich leaf mold.

Better to get off one good shot. Better to remember
     trains
derailed, turntables wrecked with plastique, raids

on the munitions dump. Better to die with a gun
in your hand you chose to pick up and had time to shoot.
Dying you pass out of choice. The others come, put up
a monument decorated with crosses, no Mogen Davids.

I come avid and omnivorous as the shining slugs.
I have eaten your history and made it myth;
among the tall trees of your pain my characters walk.
A saw whines in the valley. I say kaddish for you.

Blessed only is the act. The act of defiance,
the act of justice that fills the mouth with blood.
Blessed is the act of survival that saves the blood.
Blessed is the act of art that paints the blood

redder than real and quicker, that restores
the fallen tree to its height and birds. Memory
is the simplest form of prayer. Today you glow
like warm precious lumps of amber in my mind.

The fundamental truth

The Christian right, Islamic Jihad,
the Jewish Right Bank settlers bringing
the Messiah down, the Japanese sects
who worship by bombing subways,
they all hate each other
but more they hate the mundane,
ordinary people who love living
more than dying in radiant glory,
who shuffle and sigh and bake bread.

They need a planet of their own,
perhaps even a barren moon
with artificial atmosphere,
where they will surely be nearer
to their gods and their fiercest
enemies, where they can kill
to their heart's peace
kill to the last standing man
and leave the rest of us be.

Not mystics to whom the holy
comes in the core of struggle
in a shimmer of blinding quiet,
not scholars haggling out the inner
meaning of gnarly ancient sentences.
No, the holy comes to these zealots

as a license to kill, for self-doubt
and humility have dried like mud
under their marching feet.

They have far more in common
with each other, these braggarts
of hatred, the iron hearted
in whose ear a voice spoke
once and left them deaf.
Their faith is founded on death
of others, and everyone is other
to them, whose Torah is splattered
in letters of blood.

The hunger moon

The snow is frozen moonlight on the marshes.
How bright it is tonight, the air thin
as a skim of black ice and serrated,
cutting the lungs. My eyes sting.

Spring, I watch the moon for instruction
in planting; summer, I gauge her grasp
on the tides of the sea, the bay, my womb:
now you may gather oysters, now lay

the white, the red, the black beans
into the earth eyes rolled upward.
But winters, we are in opposition.
I must fight the strong pulls of the body.

The blood croons, curl to sleep, embryo in a seed.
Early to sleep, late to rise from the down cave.
Even at seven, night squats in the pines.
Swim in the womb of dreams and grow new limbs.

Awake at last, the body begins to crave,
not salads, not crisp apples and sweet kiwis,
but haunches of beef and thick fatty stews.
Eat, whispers the crone in the bone, eat.

The hunger moon is grinning like a skull.
The bats are asleep. The little voles

streak starving through tunnels in the snow
and voracious shrews race after them.

Eat, make fat against famine, grow round
while there's something rich to gnaw on,
urges the crone from her peasant wisdom.
She wants every woman her own pumpkin,

she wants me full as tonight's moon
when I long to wane. Why must I fight her,
who taught my mother's mother's mothers
to survive the death marches of winters past?

Tefillah

(PRAYER)

The work in this part was written for the
P'nai Or shabbat morning Siddur, Or Chadash.

Nishmat

When the night slides under with the last dimming star
and the red sky lightens between the trees,
and the heron glides tipping heavy wings in the river,
when crows stir and cry out their harsh joy,
and swift creatures of the night run toward their burrows,
and the deer raises her head and sniffs the freshening air,
and the shadows grow more distinct and then shorten,

then we rise into the day still clean as new snow.
The cat washes its paw and greets the day with gratitude.
Leviathan salutes breaching with a column of steam.
The hawk turning in the sky cries out a prayer like a
     knife.
We must wonder at the sky now thin as a speckled
     eggshell,
that now piles up its boulders of storm to crash down,
that now hangs a furry grey belly into the street.

Every day we find a new sky and a new earth
with which we are trusted like a perfect toy.
We are given the salty river of our blood
winding through us, to remember the sea and our
kindred under the waves, the hot pulsing that knocks
in our throats to consider our cousins in the grass
and the trees, all bright scattered rivulets of life.

We are given the wind within us, the breath
to shape into words that steal time, that touch
like hands and pierce like bullets, that waken

truth and deceit, sorrow and pity and joy,
that waste precious air in complaints, in lies,
in floating traps for power on the dirty air.
Yet holy breath still stretches our lungs to sing.

We are given the body, that momentary kibbutz
of elements that have belonged to frog and polar
bear, corn and oak tree, volcano and glacier.
We are lent for a time these minerals in water
and a morning every day, a morning to wake up,
rejoice and praise life in our spines, our throats,
our knees, our genitals, our brains, our tongues.

We are given fire to see against the dark,
to think, to read, to study how we are to live,
to bank in ourselves against defeat and despair
that cool and muddy our resolves, that make us forget
what we saw we must do. We are given passion
to rise like the sun in our minds with the new day
and burn the debris of habit and greed and fear.

We stand in the midst of the burning world
primed to burn with compassionate love and justice,
to turn inward and find holy fire at the core,
to turn outward and see the world that is all
of one flesh with us, see under the trash, through

the smog, the furry bee in the apple blossom,
the trout leaping, the candles our ancestors lit for us.

Fill us as the tide rustles into the reeds in the marsh.
Fill us as the rushing water overflows the pitcher.
Fill us as light fills a room with its dancing.
Let the little quarrels of the bones and the snarling
of the lesser appetites and the whining of the ego cease.
Let silence still us so you may show us your shining
and we can out of that stillness rise and praise.

S'hema

Hear, Israel, you are of G–d and G–d is one.

Praise the name that speaks us through all time.

V'ahavta

So you shall love what is holy
with all your courage, with all your passion
with all your strength.
Let the words that have come down
shine in our words and our actions.
We must teach our children to know and understand them.
We must speak about what is good
and holy within our homes
when we are working, when we are at play,
when we lie down and when we get up.
Let the work of our hands speak of goodness.
    Let it run in our blood
and glow from our doors and windows.

We should love ourselves, for we are of G–d.
We should love our neighbors as ourselves.
We should love the stranger, for we
were once strangers in the land of Egypt
and have been strangers in all the lands of the world since.
Let love fill our hearts with its clear precious water.
Heaven and earth observe how we cherish or spoil our
    world.

Heaven and earth watch whether we choose life or choose
   death.
We must choose life so our children's children may live.
Be quiet and listen to the still small
voice within that speaks in love.
Open to that voice, hear it, heed it and work for life.
Let us remember and strive to be good.
Let us remember to find what is holy
within and without.

Meditation before reading Torah

We are the people of the word
and the breath of the word fills our minds with light.
We are the people of the word
and the breath of life sings through us
playing on the pipes of our bones
and the strings of our sinews
an ancient song carved in the Laurentian granite
and new as a spring azure butterfly just drying her wings
in a moment's splash of sun.
We must live the word and make it real.

We are the people of the book
and the letters march busy as ants
carrying the work of the ages through our minds.

We are the people of the book.
Through fire and mud and dust we have borne
our scrolls tenderly as a baby swaddled in a blanket,
traveling with our words sewn in our clothes
and carried on our backs.

Let us take up the scroll of Torah
and dance with it and touch it
and read it out, for the mind
touches the word and makes it light.
So does light enter us, and we shine.

Amidah: On our feet we speak to you

We rise to speak
a web of bodies aligned like notes of music.

1.

Bless what brought us through
the sea and the fire; we are caught
in history like whales in polar ice.
Yet you have taught us to push against the walls,

to reach out and pull each other along,
to strive to find the way through
if there is no way around, to go on.
To utter ourselves with every breath

against the constriction of fear,
to know ourselves as the body born from Abraham
and Sarah, born out of rock and desert.
We reach back through two hundred arches of hips

long dust, carrying their memories inside us
to live again in our life, Isaac and Rebecca,
Rachel, Jacob, Leah. We say words shaped
by ancient use like steps worn into rock.

2.

Bless the quiet of sleep
easing over the ravaged body, who quiets

the troubled waters of the mind to a pool
in which shines the placid broad face of the moon.

Bless the teaching of how to open
in love so all the doors and windows of the body
swing wide on their rusty hinges
and we give ourselves with both hands.

Bless what stirs in us compassion
for the hunger of the chickadee in the storm
starving for seeds we can carry out,
the wounded cat wailing in the alley,

what shows us our face in a stranger,
who teaches us what we clutch shrivels
but what we give goes off in the world
carrying bread to people not yet born.

Bless the gift of memory
that breaks unbidden, released
from a flower or a cup of tea
so the dead move like rain through the room.

Bless what forces us to invent
goodness every morning and what never frees
us from the cost of knowledge, which is
to act on what we know again and again.

3.

All living are one and holy, let us remember
as we eat, as we work, as we walk and drive.

All living are one and holy, we must make ourselves worthy.
We must act out justice and mercy and healing
as the sun rises and as the sun sets,
as the moon rises and the stars wheel above us,
we must repair goodness.
We must praise the power of the one that joins us.
Whether we plunge in or thrust ourselves far out
finally we reach the face of glory too bright
for our eyes and yet we burn and we give light.

We will try to be holy,
we will try to repair the world given to us to hand on.
Precious is this treasure of words and knowledge and deeds
that moves inside us.
Holy is the hand that works for peace and for justice,
holy is the mouth that speaks for goodness,
holy is the foot that walks toward mercy.

Let us lift each other on our shoulders and carry each
    other along.
Let holiness move in us.
Let us pay attention to its small voice.
Let us see the light in others and honor that light.
Remember the dead who paid our way here dearly, dearly
and remember the unborn for whom we build our houses.

Praise the light that shines before us, through us, after us,
    Amein.

137

Kaddish

Look around us, search above us, below, behind.
We stand in a great web of being joined together.
Let us praise, let us love the life we are lent
passing through us in the body of Israel
and our own bodies, let's say amein.

Time flows through us like water.
The past and the dead speak through us.
We breathe out our children's children, blessing.

Blessed is the earth from which we grow,
blessed the life we are lent,
blessed the ones who teach us,
blessed the ones we teach,
blessed is the word that cannot say the glory
that shines through us and remains to shine
flowing past distant suns on the way to forever.
Let's say amein.

Blessed is light, blessed is darkness,
but blessed above all else is peace
which bears the fruits of knowledge
on strong branches, let's say amein.

Peace that bears joy into the world,
peace that enables love, peace over Israel
everywhere, blessed and holy is peace, let's say amein.

Havdalah

The sun slides from the sky
as the sparks of the day are tamped out.
From the last we ignite the twisted candle
that summons us to remember how to braid
into the rough wool of our daily lives
that silken skein of the bright and holy;

that reminds us we are a quilted people
who have picked up the dye of our surroundings,
as tall and short, as dark and light as the lands
we have been blown to, eating of strange
and distant trees, that we are a varied people
braided into one;

the candle that reminds us we pray with many
accents, in many languages and ways.
All are holy and burn with their own inner
light as the strands of this wax flame together.

Woman, man, whomever we love and live with,
single or coupled, webbed in family or solitary,
born a Jew or choosing, pious or searching,
we bring our thread to the pattern.
We are stronger for the weaving of our strands.

Let us draw in together before we scatter
into the maze of our jobs and worries,

let us feel ourselves in the paused dance
that is the candle with its leaping flame:
let us too pause before shabbat lets us go.

Let us rejoice in the fruit of the vine,
the blood of summer sweet and warm
on the lips, telling us, remember to enjoy
the swift innocent pleasures of the earth.

Let us breathe the perfume of the spices.
Ships sailed off the edges of maps into chaos,
tribes were enslaved and rulers overthrown
for these heady flavors more prized than gold,
now sold like flour in the market.
Let us not forget to savor the common wonders.

Let us linger in the last candlelight of shabbat.
Here we have felt ourself again a people and one.
Here we have kindled our ancestors to flame in our
    minds.
Here we have gazed on the faces of the week's casualties,
opened the doors of our guilt, raised our eyes
to the high bright places we would like to walk soon.
This little light we have borne on our braided selves—
let us take it with us cupped in our minds.

Now we drown the candle in the little lake of wine.
The only light we have kept is inside us.
Let us take it home to shine in our daily lives.

Ha-Shanah

(THE YEAR)

Shabbat moment

A scarf trailing
over the lilac sunset,
fair weather clouds,
cirrus uncinus
silk chiffon.
Twilight softens the air,
whispering, come,
lie down with me.

Untie the knots of the will.
Loosen
your clenched grip
barren hills of bone.
Here, no edges to hone,
only the palm fallen
open as a rose about
to toss its petals.

What you have made,
what you have spoiled
let go.
Let twilight empty
the crowded rooms
quiet the jostling colors

to hues of swirling water
pearls of fog.

This is the time
for letting time go
like a released balloon
dwindling.
Tilt your neck and let
your face open to the sky
like a pond catching light
drinking the darkness.

At the New Moon: Rosh Hodesh

Once a two day holiday, the most sacred stretches
in the slow swing of the epicycling year;
then a remnant, a half holiday for women,
a little something to keep us less unsatisfied;
then abandoned at enlightenment along with herbals
and amulets, bobbeh mysehs, grandmothers' stories.

Now we fetch it up from the bottom of the harbor,
a bone on which the water has etched itself,
and from this bone we fashion a bird, extinct
and never yet born, evolving feathers
from our hair, blood from our salt, strength
from our backs, vision from our brains.

Fly out over the city, dove of the light,
owl of the moon, for we are weaving your wings
from our longings, diaphanous and bony.
Pilots and rabbis soared. The only females
to fly were witches and demons, the power
to endure and the power to destroy alone

granted us. But we too can invent,
can make, can do, undo. Here we stand
in a circle, the oldest meeting, the shape
women assume when we come together
that echoes ours, the flower, the mouth,
breast, opening, pool, the source.

We greet the moon that is not gone
but only hidden, unreflecting, inturned
and introspective, gathering strength to grow

as we greet the first slim nail paring
of her returning light. Don't we understand
the strength that wells out of retreat?

Can we not learn to turn in to our circle,
to sink into the caves of our silence,
to drink lingering by those deep cold wells,
to dive into the darkness of the heart's storm
until under the crashing surge of waves
it is still except for our slow roaring breath?

We need a large pattern of how things change
that shows us not a straight eight-lane tearing
through hills blasted into bedrock; not stairs
mounting to the sacrificial pyramid where hearts
are torn out to feed the gods of power, but the coil
of the moon, that epicycling wheel

that grows fat and skinny, advances and withers,
four steps forward and three back, and yet nothing
remains the same, for the mountains are piled up
and worn down, for the rivers eat into the stone
and the fields blow away and the sea makes sand
spits and islands and carries off the dune.

Let the half day festival of the new moon
remind us how to retreat and grow strong, how to
reflect and learn, how to push our bellies forward,
how to roll and turn and pull the tides up, up
when we need them, how to come back each time
we look dead, making a new season shine.

146

Wellfleet shabbat

The hawk eye of the sun slowly shuts.
The breast of the bay is softly feathered
dove grey. The sky is barred like the sand
when the tide trickles out.

The great doors of shabbat are swinging
open over the ocean, loosing the moon
floating up slow   distorted   vast   a copper
balloon just sailing free.

The wind slides over the waves, patting
them with its giant hand, and the sea
stretches its muscles in the deep,
purrs and rolls over.

The sweet beeswax candles flicker
and sigh, standing between the phlox
and the roast chicken. The wine shines
its red lantern of joy.

Here on this piney sandspit, the Shekinah
comes on the short strong wings of the seaside
sparrow raising her song and bringing
down the fresh clean night.

The head of the year

The moon is dark tonight, a new
moon for a new year. It is
hollow and hungers to be full.
It is the black zero of beginning.

Now you must void yourself
of injuries, insults, incursions.
Go with empty hands to those
you have hurt and make amends.

It is not too late. It is early
and about to grow. Now
is the time to do what you
know you must and have feared

to begin. Your face is dark
too as you turn inward to face
yourself, the hidden twin
of all you must grow to be.

Forgive the dead year. Forgive
yourself. What will be wants
to push through your fingers.
The light you seek hides

in your belly. The light you
crave longs to stream from
your eyes. You are the moon
that will wax in new goodness.

Tashlich

Go to the ocean and throw the crumbs in,
all that remains of seven years.
When you wept, didn't I taste your tears
on my cheek, give you bread for salt?

Here where I sing at full pitch
and volume uncensored, I was attacked.
The pale sister nibbled like a mouse
in the closets with sharp pointy teeth.

She let herself in with her own key.
My trust garlanded her round. Indeed
it was convenient to trust her
while she waned paper thin with envy.

Here she coveted. Here she crept.
Here her cold fluttering hands lingered
on secrets and dipped into the honey.
Her shadow fell on the contents of every drawer.

Alone in the house she made love
to herself in the mirror wearing
stolen gowns; then she carried them home
for their magic to color her life.

Little losses spread like tooth decay.

Furtive betrayals festered, cysts
hidden in flesh. Her greed swelled
in the dark, its hunger always roaring.

No number of gifts could silence
those cries of resentful hunger,
not for the baubles, the scarves,
the blouses she stole, but to be twenty

and pretty again, not to have to work
to live but merely to be blond and thin
and let men happen like rain in the night
and never to wake alone.

On the new year my grandmother Hannah
told me to carry crumbs to the water
and cast them out. We are tossing
away the bad part of ourselves

and we are throwing evil from the house
the rancid taint of envy spoiling the food
the pricing fingers of envy rumpling the cloth
the secret ill wisher chewing from inside

the heart's red apple to rot it out.
I cast you away like spoiled milk.
Let the salty wind air the house and cleanse
the stain of betrayal from the new year.

Breadcrumbs

Some time on Rosh Hashanah I go,
a time dictated by tide charts,
services. The once I did tashlich

on the rising tide and the crumbs
floated back to me, my energy soured,
vinegar of anxiety. Now I eye the times.

I choose the dike, where the Herring River
pours in and out of the bay, where at
low tide in September blue herons stalk

totemic to spear the alewives hastening
silver-sided from the fresh ponds to
the sea. As I toss my crumbs, muttering

prayers, a fisherman rebukes me: It's
not right to feed the fish, it distracts
them from his bait. Sometimes

it's odd to be a Jew, like a three-
legged heron with bright purple head,
an ibis in white plumes diving

except that with global warming
we do sometimes glimpse an ibis

in our marshes, and I am rooted here

to abide the winter when this tourist
has gone back to Cincinnati.
My rituals are mated to this fawn

colored land floating on the horizon
of water. My havurah calls itself
Am ha-Yam, people of the sea,

and we are wedded to the ocean
as truly as the Venetian doge who tossed
his gold ring to the Adriatic.

All rivers flow at last into the sea
but here it is, at once. So we stand
the tourist casting for his fish

and I tossing my bread. The fish
snap it up. Tonight perhaps
he will broil my sins for supper.

The New Year of the Trees

It is the New Year of the Trees, but here
the ground is frozen under the crust of snow.
The trees snooze, their buds tight as nuts.
Rhododendron leaves roll up their stiff scrolls.

In the white and green north of the diaspora
I am stirred by a season that will not arrive
for six weeks, as wines on far continents prickle
to bubbles when their native vines bloom.

What blossoms here are birds jostling
at feeders, pecking sunflower seeds
and millet through the snow: tulip red
cardinal, daffodil finch, larkspur jay,

the pansybed of sparrows and juncos, all hungry.
They too are planters of trees, spreading seeds
of favorites along fences. On the earth closed
to us all as a book in a language we cannot

yet read, the seeds, the bulbs, the eggs
of the fervid green year await release.
Over them on February's cold table I spread
a feast. Wings rustle like summer leaves.

Beytzeh: Season of the egg

It's the season of the egg,
older than any named creed:
that perfect shape that signs
a pregnant woman, the moon

slightly compressed, as if
a great serpent held it
in its opened mouth
to carry or eat.

Eggs smell funky
slipped from under
the hen's breast, hotter
than our blood.

Christians paint them;
we roast them. The only
time in the whirling year
I ever eat roasted egg:

a campfire flavor, bit
burnt, reeking of haste
like the matzoh there was no
time to let rise.

We like our eggs honest,
brown. Outside my window

the chickadees choose partners
to lay tiny round eggs.

The egg of the world cracks
raggedly open and the wet
scraggly chick of northern
spring emerges gaunt, dripping.

Soon it will preen its green
feathers, soon it will grow
fat and strong, its wings
blue and blinding.

Tonight we dip the egg in salt
water like bowls of tears.
Elijah comes with the fierce
early spring bringing prophecy

that cracks open the head
swollen with importance.
Every day there is more work
to do and stronger light.

Charoset

Sweet and sticky
I always make too much
at Pesach so I have
an excuse to eat you
all week.

Moist and red
the female treat
nothing at all like clay
for bricks, nothing
like mortar.

No, you are sweet as
a mouth kissing,
you are fragrant
with cinnamon
spicy as havdalah boxes.

Don't go on too long,
you whisper sweetly.
Heed the children
growing restive, their
bellies growling.

You speak of pleasure
in the midst of remembered pain.

You offer the first taste
of the meal, promising joy
like a picnic on a stone

where long ago an ancestor
was buried, too long
ago to weep. We nod
and remembering is enough
to offer, like honey.

If much of what we must
recall is bitter, you
are the reminder that
joy too lights its candles
tonight in the mind.

Zeroah: Lamb shank

It grosses out many of my friends.
They don't eat meat, let alone
place it on a ritual platter.
I am not so particular, or more so.

Made of flesh and bone, liver
and sinew, salty blood and brain,
I know they weren't ghosts who trekked
out of baked mud huts into the desert.

Blood was spilled, red and real:
first ours, then theirs. Blood
splashed on the doorposts proclaimed
in danger the rebellion within.

We are pack and herd animals.
One Jew is not a Jew, but we are
a people together, plural, joined.
We were made flesh and we bled.

And we fled, under the sign
of the slaughtered lamb to live
and die for each other. We are
meat that thinks and sings.

Maror

A bitter cud.
Biting into the bitter, that bites back.
Of all the gross tastes, sweet and salty,
sour, we seek it the least.
We spit it out. But not tonight.

Tonight we must taste our bitterness.
Bite into our failure, suck its essence.
We were slaves in Egypt, the Haggadah
reminds us, and we still are,
but who enslaves us to what?

The bone we chew is our own.
Only I can tell myself where
I am caught, trapped, held
fast, bored but comfortable
in the box I know so well.

This is the moment for naming
that box, for feeling the walls,
for studying the dimensions
of the prison I must choose
to leave in my exodus of one.

I can join with no one else,
I cannot walk out with you

until I measure my walls
then break them down.
Darkness into light.

Fear and silence into
cursing. The known
abandoned for something
new and frightening. Bitter
is the first taste of freedom.

Karpas

I am one of those weird people
who eat the parsley garnish
off restaurant dinners, not
only mine but yours and his.
I will nibble them all.

I like the sharp almost
gritty bite of the leaves,
its formidable green,
its prickly rank scent,
its persistence under snow.

Dip the leaves curly
as pubic hairs into the tears
in the bowl, remembering
old pain and the strength
to endure and grow on.

An herb whose white root
grows down and down into the earth,
so that gardeners say it goes
to the devil twice
before it stretches up,

slow to germinate, slow growing
and then weedy and stubborn,

surviving drought, neglect,
frost, the iron weight of winter.
Its leaves dipped in salt water

give the taste of spring—not
the sentimental spring of bunnies
and florists' bouquets, but real
season of hungry deer and geese
honking tiny in the grey sky,

of dirt thawing with the bones
of winter exposed to the sun,
old deaths and the cost
of survival, the miracle
of days growing longer like hair.

Chazeret: Lettuce in rebellion

Bland almost as water,
you are meek and prolific as mice.
You are the carrier of sharp news,
a pretense for dressing you up,
a hanger, a clothes horse,
but with a certain shy sweetness.

You sit there demurely in the garden
rows with almost no pests.
Then one day you stick up
a tower of leaves
and turn bitter overnight,
sculptured, tall, inedible.

You have escaped us:
our sharp teeth and our salad
bowls, our sandwiches and rolls.
Instead like a green rocket you rise
hot and spiky, joyfully bitter
waving your own new flag.

Matzoh

Flat you are as a door mat
and as homely.
No crust, no glaze, you lack
a cosmetic glow.
You break with a snap.
You are dry as a twig
split from an oak
in midwinter.
You are bumpy as a mud basin
in a drought.
Square as a slab of pavement,
you have no inside
to hide raisins or seeds.
You are pale as the full moon
pocked with craters.

What we see is what we get,
honest, plain, dry
shining with nostalgia
as if baked with light
instead of heat.
The bread of flight and haste
in the mouth you
promise, home.

Salt water

It is a bowl of tears on the table
into which we dip the parsley,
into which we dip the egg.

It is a miniature ocean on the table,
salt as the Sea of Reeds through
which they were to pass

not to safety (never safety)
but to where they were promised
they would if they chose be free.

It is the salt water of our sweat
pressed through our skin
as the body labors, for we are bidden

not only to rest on the seventh day
but work on the others, and the brain
too in its fever of creation exudes.

Salt like the sea, salt like our blood
salt like the waters of the womb:
the salt of regret and the salt of effort.

Maggid

The courage to let go of the door, the handle.
The courage to shed the familiar walls whose very
stains and leaks are comfortable as the little moles
of the upper arm; stains that recall a feast,
a child's naughtiness, a loud blattering storm
that slapped the roof hard, pouring through.

The courage to abandon the graves dug into the hill,
the small bones of children and the brittle bones
of the old whose marrow hunger had stolen;
the courage to desert the tree planted and only
begun to bear; the riverside where promises were
shaped; the street where their empty pots were broken.

The courage to leave the place whose language you
    learned
as early as your own, whose customs however dan-
gerous or demeaning, bind you like a halter
you have learned to pull inside, to move your load;
the land fertile with the blood spilled on it;
the roads mapped and annotated for survival.

The courage to walk out of the pain that is known
into the pain that cannot be imagined,
mapless, walking into the wilderness, going
barefoot with a canteen into the desert;

stuffed in the stinking hold of a rotting ship
sailing off the map into dragons' mouths,

Cathay, India, Siberia, goldeneh medina,
leaving bodies by the way like abandoned treasure.
So they walked out of Egypt. So they bribed their way
out of Russia under loads of straw; so they steamed
out of the bloody smoking charnelhouse of Europe
on overloaded freighters forbidden all ports—

out of pain into death or freedom or a different
painful dignity, into squalor and politics.
We Jews are all born of wanderers, with shoes
under our pillows and a memory of blood that is ours
raining down. We honor only those Jews who changed
tonight, those who chose the desert over bondage

who walked into the strange and became strangers
and gave birth to children who could look down
on them standing on their shoulders for having
been slaves. We honor those who let go of every-
thing but freedom, who ran, who revolted, who fought,
who became other by saving themselves.

Summer mourning

One summer morning the light pools heavy
with exhaust fumes on the dying grass;
every leaf on every tree bears the marks
of gnawing, of the teeth of caterpillars,
or is soiled with brown rot or fuzzy mold;
in dawn's yellow rose, the Japanese beetle
has chewed and shat and now couples in bronze.
There is a time when summer rusts like wheat.

In the fullness of the melon moon the void
of new moon coils like a seed; in the ripeness
of harvest we mourn failure and almost-beens.
Tishah b'Av. With the feast comes mourning
for as the year slides down from its fiery peak
the spiral of other summers and other years
unwinds ghostly behind. Sometimes the heat
and the humidity feel like inertia

and I struggle against history as a fly
caught on flypaper: swimming in molasses.
Sometimes history seems to me the bad air
in a tunnel where I am trapped in rush hour
traffic, all these cars at one time stalled
pumping out poison, one angry person in each

drumming their fingers on the steering wheel
and longing for teleportation.

How many marriages choke on their own debris,
the habits of old anger, an arthritis
disabling motion. Ancient injustices
still leak their poison into the water table
while new ones irradiate the skulls of embryos.
Tishah b'Av. I know how the cost of change
cuts down to the living bone; and how the cost
of what is, is the bone rotting from within.

Coming up on September

White butterflies, with single
black fingerpaint eyes on their wings,
dart and settle, eddy and mate
over the green tangle of vines
in Labor Day morning steam.

The year grinds into ripeness
and rot, grapes darkening,
pears yellowing, the first
Virginia creeper twining crimson,
the grasses, dry straw to burn.

The New Year rises, beckoning
across the umbrellas on the sand.
I begin to reconsider my life.
What is the yield of my impatience?
What is the fruit of my resolve?

I turn from my frantic white dance
over the jungle of productivity
and slowly a niggun slides,
cold water down my throat.
I rest on a leaf spotted red.

Now is the time to let the mind
search backwards like the raven loosed

to see what can feed us. Now,
the time to cast the mind forward
to chart an aerial map of the months.

The New Year is a great door
that stands across the evening and Yom
Kippur is the second door. Between them
are song and silence, stone and clay pot
to be filled from within myself.

I will find there both ripeness and rot,
what I have done and undone,
what I must let go with the waning days
and what I must take in. With the last
tomatoes, we harvest the fruit of our lives.

The ram's horn sounding

1.

Giant porcupine, I walk a rope braided
of my intestines and veins, beige and blue and red,
while clutched in my arms, you lie glaring
sore eyed, snuffling and sticking your spines at me.

Always I am finding quills worked into some unsuspected
muscle, an innocent pillow of fat pierced by you.
We sleep in the same bed nightly and you take it all.
I wake shuddering with cold, the quilt stripped from me.

No, not a porcupine: a leopard cub.
Beautiful you are as light and as darkness.
Avid, fierce, demanding with sharp teeth
to be fed and tended, you only want my life.

Ancient, living, a deep and tortuous river
that rose in the stark mountains beyond the desert,
you have gouged through rocks with slow persistence
enduring, meandering in long shining coils to the sea.

2.

A friend who had been close before being recruited
by the CIA once sent me a postcard of the ghetto at
    Tetuán
yellowed like old pornography numbered 17,

a prime number as one might say a prime suspect.

The photographer stood well clear of the gate
to shoot old clothes tottering in the tight street,
beards matted and holy with grease,
children crooked under water jugs,
old men austere and busy as hornets.
Flies swarmed on the lens.
Dirt was the color.

Oh, I understood your challenge.
My Jewishness seemed to you sentimental,
perverse, planned obsolescence.
Paris was hot and dirty the night I first
met relatives who had survived the war.
My identity squatted whining on my arm
gorging itself on my thin blood.
A gaggle of fierce insistent speakers of ten
languages had different passports mother
from son, brother from sister, had four
passports all forged, kept passports
from gone countries (Transylvania, Bohemia,
old despotisms fading like Victorian wallpaper),
were used to sewing contraband into coat
linings. I smuggled for them across two borders.

Their wars were old ones.
Mine was just starting.

Old debater, it's easy in any manscape
to tell the haves from the have-nots.
Any ghetto is a Klein bottle.
You think you are outside gazing idly in.
Winners write history; losers
die of it, like the plague.

3.

A woman and a Jew, sometimes more
of a contradiction than I can sweat out,
yet finally the intersection that is both
collision and fusion, stone and seed.

Like any poet I wrestle the holy name
and know there is no wording finally
can map, constrain or summon that fierce
voice whose long wind lifts my hair

chills my skin and fills my lungs
to bursting. I serve the word
I cannot name, who names me daily,
who speaks me out by whispers and shouts.

Coming to the new year, I am picked
up like the ancient ram's horn to sound

over the congregation of people and beetles,
of pines, whales, marshhawks and asters.

Then I am dropped into the factory of words
to turn my little wheels and grind my own
edges, back on piece work again, knowing
there is no justice we don't make daily

like bread and love. Shekinah,
stooping on hawk wings prying into my heart
with your silver beak; floating down
a milkweed silk dove of sunset;

riding the filmy sheets of rain like a ghost
ship with all sails still unfurled;
bless me and use me for telling and naming
the forever collapsing shades and shapes of life,

the rainbows cast across our eyes by the moment
of sun, the shadows we trail across the grass
running, the opal valleys of the night flesh,
the moments of knowledge ripping into the brain

and aligning everything into a new pattern
as a constellation learned organizes blur
into stars, the blood kinship with all green, hairy
and scaled folk born from the ancient warm sea.

Some of the poems new to this collection originally appeared in the following publications:

Caprice: "The real hearth"

Chiron Review: "The aunt I wanted to be"

Connecticut Review: "Marriage in winter"

Footwork: The Patterson Literary Review: "One bird, if there is only one, dies in the night"

Jewish Women's Literary Annual: "Charoset"

Kalliope: "The rabbi's granddaughter and the Christmas tree" and "What she craved"

Kerem: "Snowflakes, my mother called them"

Lunar Calendar: "The head of the year"

The Montserrat Review: "On shabbat she dances in the candle flames"

P'nai Or Siddur: "S'hema," "Meditation before reading Torah," and "Havdalah"

Prairie Schooner: "Karpas"

The Southern California Anthology: "The wicked stepmother"

Tikkun: "Learning to read," "The ark of consequence," and "The fundamental truth"; will be publishing "Zeroah: Lamb shank," "Chazeret: Lettuce in rebellion," and "Salt water"

Verve: "In the grip of the solstice" and "Woman in a shoe"

Many of the poems in this volume are from the following previously published books:

Available Light, copyright © 1988 by Middlemarsh, Inc.; published by Alfred A. Knopf, Inc.

Circles on the Water, copyright © 1963, 1964, 1965, 1966, 1967, 1968, 1969, 1971, 1972, 1973, 1974, 1975, 1976, 1978, 1979, 1980, 1982 by Marge Piercy; published by Alfred A. Knopf, Inc.

Hard Loving, copyright © 1969; published by Wesleyan University Press.

A NOTE ABOUT THE TYPE

The text of this book was set in Minister, a typeface designed by
M. Fahrenwaldt for the German Schriftguss foundry in 1929. A modern
interpretation of the classic Venetian letterforms of the fifteenth century,
Minister is characterized by a calligraphic spirit, well-defined concave-
shaped serifs, and broadly formed capital letters.

Composed by NK Graphics, Keene, New Hampshire
Printed and bound by Quebecor Printing, Fairfield, Pennsylvania
Calligraphy by Carole Lowenstein
Designed by Robert C. Olsson